SECOND EDITION

1

INSIDE READING

The Academic Word List in Context

Arline Burgmeier

SERIES DIRECTOR:

Cheryl Boyd Zimmerman

OXFORD
UNIVERSITY PRESS

OXFORD
UNIVERSITY PRESS

198 Madison Avenue
New York, NY 10016 USA

Great Clarendon Street, Oxford, OX2 6DP, United Kingdom

Oxford University Press is a department of the University of Oxford.
It furthers the University's objective of excellence in research, scholarship,
and education by publishing worldwide. Oxford is a registered trade
mark of Oxford University Press in the UK and in certain other countries

General Manager, American ELT: Laura Pearson
Publisher: Stephanie Karras
Associate Publishing Manager: Sharon Sargent
Development Editor: Keyana Shaw
Director, ADP: Susan Sanguily
Executive Design Manager: Maj-Britt Hagsted
Electronic Production Manager: Julie Armstrong
Senior Designer: Yin Ling Wong
Designer: Jessica Balaschak
Image Manager: Trisha Masterson
Production Coordinator: Brad Tucker

ISBN: 978 0 19 441627 6 STUDENT BOOK

Printed in China

This book is printed on paper from certified and well-managed sources

ACKNOWLEDGEMENTS

*The authors and publisher are grateful to those who have given permission to reproduce
the following extracts and adaptations of copyright material:*

Illustrations by: p4 Infomen (timeline); p10 Infomen; p19 Infomen; p27
Jonathan Williams; p28 Infomen; p41 Infomen; p51 Infomen (advert); p67
Infomen; p73 Jonathan Williams; p91 Infomen; p113 Infomen; p122 Infomen;
p131 Infomen (chart).

*We would also like to thank the following for permission to reproduce the following
photographs:* Cover: Elosoenpersona Photo/Getty Images (bike); LEROY Francis/
Getty Images (boat); Jeff Hunter/Getty Images (fish); Ann Cutting/Getty
Images (magnifying glass); Glow Images/Getty Images (fruit loops); Dorling
Kindersley/Getty Images (penny farthing); Marilyn Volan/Shutterstock
(diamonds); Dawid Zagorski/Shutterstock); Jitka Volfova/Shutterstock; pg.
xii, Marcin Krygier / iStockphoto (laptop); p1 James Nazz/Oxford University
Press; p3 Gary Ombler/Getty Images; p4 Melissa Farlow/Getty Images (penny-
farthing); p11 Sean Gallup/Getty Images; p17 Kletr/Shutterstock; p18 Kletr/
Shutterstock; p20 MARKA /Alamy; p26 Gianni Dagli Orti/Corbis UK Ltd.; p33
LittleMiss/Shutterstock; p34 Ken Welsh/Alamy; p35 Yuri Arcurs/Shutterstock;
p43 NAN728/Shutterstock; p44 imagebroker/Alamy; p49 Mike Flippo/
Shutterstock; p51 epa european pressphoto agency b.v./Alamy (handshake);
p52 Rex Features; p58 Mark Scott/Getty Images; p59 Paylessimages/Fotolia;
p60 Gabriela Hasbun/Getty Images; p65 Kuzmin Andrey/Shutterstock;
p66 Steve Cukrov/Shutterstock; p68 Roberto Westbrook / Blend Images /
Superstock Ltd.; p74 Golden Pixels LLC/Shutterstock (meeting); p74 Tim
Tadder/Corbis UK Ltd. (musician); p81 Chernetskiy/Shutterstock; p82
Pinosub/Shutterstock; p83 Pablo Paul/Alamy (window); p83 Alexander Raths/
Shutterstock (scientists); p89 Photos 12/Alamy; p90 Brand X Pictures/Oxford
University Press; p97 Brand Z/Oxford University Press; p98 George Heyer/Getty
Images; p99 Robert Landau/Corbis UK Ltd. (Macdonalds); p99 Everett Kennedy
Brown/epa/Corbis UK Ltd. (Mos); p105 akg-images; p106 Emile Wamsteker/
Getty Images (mall); p106 Kevin Foy/Alamy (shop); p114 John Phillips/
Photofusion Picture Library; p115 Karen Huntt/Corbis UK Ltd.; p116 Andrew
Fox/Alamy; p121 Jason LaVeris/Getty Images; p123 michaeljung/Shutterstock;
p129 Bill Frische/Shutterstock; p130 Patrick Frilet/Rex Features; p131 Danita
Delimont/Getty Images (sea); p137 Henry Groskinsky/Time & Life Pictures/
Getty Images; p138 P Rona/OAR/National Undersea Research Program/NOAA
/Science Photo Library (vent); p138 B. Murton/Southampton Oceanography
Centre/Science Photo Library (anenome); p145 Africa Studio/Shutterstock;
p146 Dawid Zagorski/Shutterstock; p147 Culver Pictures, Inc./Superstock Ltd.
(trumpet); p147 Alexandr Mitiuc/Fotolia (teeth); p154 Photos 12/Alamy; p155
MARK GILLILAND/AP/Press Association Images; p156 Win McNamee/Getty
Images; Inside front cover: Rüstem Gürler/iStockphoto (iMac); Stephen Krow/
iStockphoto (iPhone).

Acknowledgements

We would like to acknowledge the following individuals for their input during the development of the series:

Amina Saif Mohammed Al Hashamia
College of Applied Sciences – Nizwa, Oman

Amal Al Muqarshi
College of Applied Sciences – Ibri, Oman

Dr. Gail Al-Hafidh
Sharjah Women's College –
Higher Colleges of Technology, U.A.E.

Saleh Khalfan Issa Al-Rahbi
College of Applied Sciences – Nizwa, Oman

Chris Alexis
College of Applied Sciences – Sur, Oman

Bernadette Anayah
Folsom Lake College, CA, U.S.A.

Paul Blomeyer
King Fahd Naval Academy, Jubail,
Kingdom of Saudi Arabia

Judith Buckman
College of Applied Sciences – Salalah, Oman

Peter Bull
Abu Dhabi Men's College –
Higher Colleges of Technology, U.A.E.

Bjorn Candel
Fujairah Men's College –
Higher Colleges of Technology, U.A.E

Geraldine Chell
Sharjah Women's College –
Higher Colleges of Technology, U.A.E

Hui-chen Chen
Shi-lin High School of Commerce, Taipei

Kim Dammers
Golden Bridge Educational Centre, Mongolia

Steven John Donald
Waikato Institute of Education, New Zealand

Patricia Gairaud
San Jose City College, CA, U.S.A.

Joyce Gatto
College of Lake County, IL, U.S.A.

Sally Gearhart
Santa Rosa Junior College, CA, U.S.A.

Dr. Simon Green
Colleges of Applied Sciences, Oman

Andrew Hirst
Sharjah Women's College –
Higher Colleges of Technology, U.A.E

Elena Hopkins
Delaware County Community College, DE, U.S.A.

William Hussain
College of Applied Sciences – Sur, Oman

Tom Johnson
Abu Dhabi Men's College –
Higher Colleges of Technology, U.A.E.

Sei-Hwa Jung
Catholic University of Korea, South Korea

Graham Martindale
SHCT Sharjah Higher –
Colleges of Technology, U.A.E.

Mary McKee
Abu Dhabi Men's College –
Higher Colleges of Technology, U.A.E.

Lisa McMurray
Abu Dhabi Men's College –
Higher Colleges of Technology, U.A.E.

Sally McQuinn
Fujairah Women's College –
Higher Colleges of Technology, U.A.E.

Hsieh Meng-Tsung
National Cheng Kung University, Tainan

Marta Mueller
Folsom Lake College, RCC, CA, U.S.A.

Zekariya Özşevik
Middle East Technical University, Turkey

Margaret Plenert
California State University, Fullerton UEE,
American Language Program, CA, U.S.A.

Dorothy Ramsay
College of Applied Sciences –
Sohar, Oman

Cindy Roiland
College of Lake County, IL, U.S.A.

Elia Sarah
State University of New York
at New Paltz, NY, U.S.A.

Rachel Scott
Sharjah Women's College –
Higher Colleges of Technology, U.A.E.

Tony Sexton
Abu Dhabi Men's College –
Higher Colleges of Technology, U.A.E.

Siân Walters
Sharjah Men's College –
Higher Colleges of Technology, U.A.E.

Martin Weatherby
St. Thomas University, Japan

Contents

Unit 1 Riding Through History   1

Content Area: Engineering

Unit 2 Fighting Diseases   17

Content Area: Medicine

Unit 3 They Know What You Want   33

Content Area: Marketing

Unit 4 Identifying People   49

Content Area: Sociology

Unit 5 Success Story   65

Content Area: Psychology

An Insider's Guide to Academic Reading

Develop reading skills and aquire the Academic Word List with
Inside Reading Second Edition.

Student Books

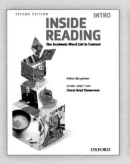   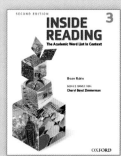 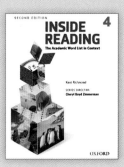

iTools for all levels

  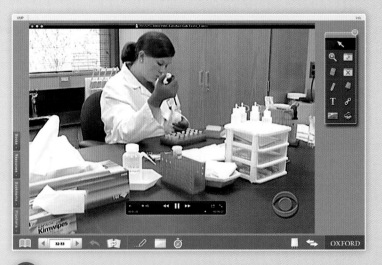

Authentic video available on iTools and the Student Website.

Getting Started

Each unit in *Inside Reading* features

> **Two high-interest reading texts** from an academic content area
> **Reading skills** relevant to the academic classroom
> Targeted words from the **Academic Word List**

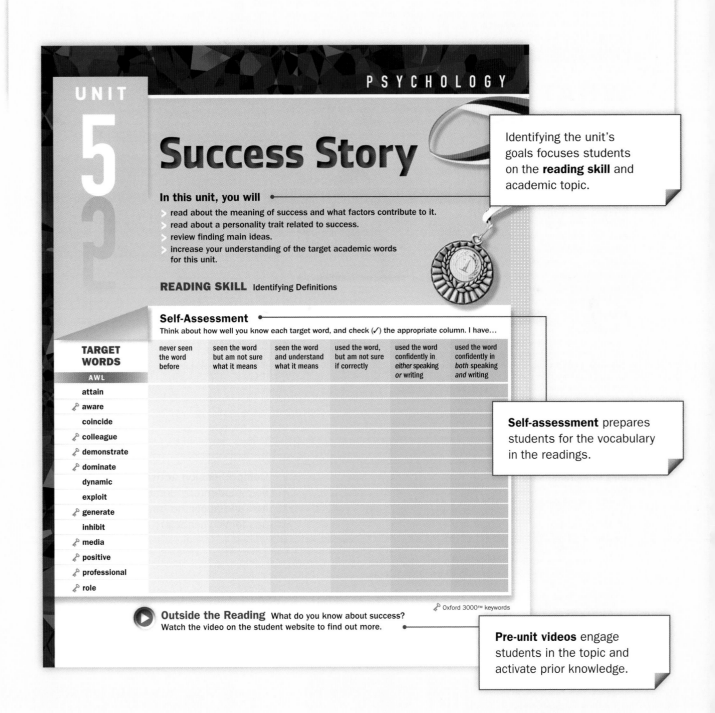

PSYCHOLOGY

UNIT

5

Success Story

In this unit, you will

> read about the meaning of success and what factors contribute to it.
> read about a personality trait related to success.
> review finding main ideas.
> increase your understanding of the target academic words for this unit.

READING SKILL Identifying Definitions

Identifying the unit's goals focuses students on the **reading skill** and academic topic.

Self-Assessment
Think about how well you know each target word, and check (✓) the appropriate column. I have…

TARGET WORDS	never seen the word before	seen the word but am not sure what it means	seen the word and understand what it means	used the word, but am not sure if correctly	used the word confidently in *either* speaking *or* writing	used the word confidently in *both* speaking *and* writing
AWL						
attain						
aware						
coincide						
colleague						
demonstrate						
dominate						
dynamic						
exploit						
generate						
inhibit						
media						
positive						
professional						
role						

Self-assessment prepares students for the vocabulary in the readings.

Outside the Reading What do you know about success? Watch the video on the student website to find out more.

🔑 Oxford 3000™ keywords

Pre-unit videos engage students in the topic and activate prior knowledge.

High-interest Texts

Before You Read

Read these questions. Discuss your answers in a small group.

1. How would you define success?
2. Are all famous people successful? Are all successful people famous? Give examples to support your opinion.
3. Name some people you consider successful. Why do you consider them successful?

> **Discussion questions activate students' knowledge** and prepare them to read.

◉ Read

This article discusses important information about how to be successful. It defines success and explains what it takes to achieve it.

WHAT IS SUCCESS?

What is success? is it wealth? Fame? Power? We tend to think of success as something unusual, something that requires special talents to achieve. That's
5 because stories in the **media** about successful business executives, **professional** golfers, glamorous movie stars, best-selling authors, and powerful politicians lead us to believe that only a few special people are successful. We may
10 not hear about them, but ordinary people can be successful, too. Success is about reaching for something—and getting it. It is about having something you didn't have before. It is about **attaining** something that is valued by others.

Success requires ambition and hard work.

> **High-interest readings** motivate students.

> **Academic Word List vocabulary** is presented in context.

SETTING GOALS
15 Success begins with a clear goal, and **attaining** that goal requires ambition. Ambition is the energy that drives people to work hard, to learn more, and to seek opportunities to advance themselves. Some people have a clear goal, but they lack the ambition to make their dream come true. Other people have great ambition but no

Reading Comprehension

A. Mark each sentence as *T* (True) or *F* (False) according to the information in Reading 1. Use your dictionary to check the meaning of new words.

___ 1. Stories generated by the media demonstrate that ordinary people can be successful.

___ 2. Family plays a major role in influencing a child's level of ambition.

___ 3. The teen years often coincide with a fear of failure and a lack of ambition.

___ 4. Positive learning experiences in the early years can inhibit persistence.

___ 5. Dynamic people are aware that they must take effective action to attain success.

___ 6. Despite their backgrounds, professional people are the most likely to succeed.

___ 7. Meeting the needs of today may dominate the thoughts of a young adult who grew up in a poor family.

___ 8. People seeking success might ask colleagues to assist them.

___ 9. One way to prepare for success is to exploit opportunities to learn through observation.

> **Comprehension activities** help students understand the text and apply the targeted academic vocabulary.

Explicit Reading Skill Instruction

READING SKILL Identifying Time and Sequence Words

LEARN

Understanding the *order of events* in a story is often essential for understanding the story, especially a mystery such as Reading 1. The order of events can be shown in several ways:

1. Sentences in a paragraph usually describe actions in the order that they happened.
2. Time words such as *Monday, March, summer,* or *1989* tell when actions took place.
3. Words such as *before, after, soon, first, next, meanwhile, then, finally,* and *subsequently* can show the order of events.
4. Phrases such as *three days later, the next year,* and *at the same time* also show time order.

APPLY

A. With a partner, use time clues and logic to figure out the order in which these events in Reading 1 took place. Number them from *1* to *9*.

___ A detective arrives.

___ The tall man hears voices downstairs.

___ Susan calls the police.

___ Susan realizes they have forgotten their tickets.

___ The tall man watches Susan and Eduard drive off.

___ Eduard tells the servant how to open the safe.

___ The tall man stuffs the jewelry into the red bag.

___ Susan concludes that someone is inside.

___ The tall man climbs out of the window.

> **Explicit reading skills** provide the foundation for effective, critical reading.

> **Practice exercises** enable students to implement new reading skills successfully.

READING SKILL Identifying Time and Sequence Words

APPLY

A. Scan the first four paragraphs of Reading 2. Answer the questions in complete sentences. Include the time words or phrases used in the Reading.

1. When did Sherlock Holmes do his detective work?

2. When do the police send an ME and a CSI team?

3. When do the CSIs take photographs in relation to other tasks?

B. Number these tasks from *1* to *7*, in the order in which they are done by the CSI team.

___ dust objects for fingerprints

___ take photographs

___ send evidence to a forensics laboratory

___ present their evidence in a court of law

___ look for drops of blood or strands of hair

___ label the evidence

___ consult with the police chief

REVIEW A SKILL Identifying Examples (See pp. 52–53)

What kind of examples are listed in paragraph 4?

_____

What kind of examples are listed in paragraph 5?

_____

> **Recycling of reading skills** allows students to apply knowledge in new contexts.

The Academic Word List in Context

Based on a corpus of 3.4 million words, the **Academic Word List (AWL)** is the most principled and widely accepted list of academic words. Compiled by Averil Coxhead in 2000, it was informed by academic materials across the academic disciplines.

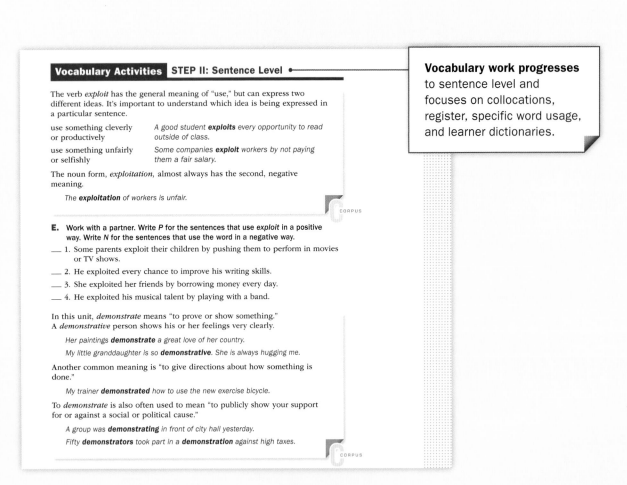

Vocabulary Activities STEP I: Word Level

A. Use the target vocabulary in the box to complete this story. Use the words in parentheses to help you.

attained	dominant	positive
coincided with	dynamic	professional
demonstrated	generating	was aware

As a boy, Lance Armstrong excelled in many sports. By his teen years, however, bicycling had become the _____ interest in his life. He easily won
(1. most important)
many local cycling races. But his goal was to be a _____ racer. In his
(2. paid)
first race, he finished last of 111 riders. He was discouraged and almost quit racing. Instead, he trained harder and soon _____ the rank of number one
(3. reached)
bicyclist in the world. But his success _____ a terrible illness. Lance,
(4. happened at the same time as)
just 25 years old, was diagnosed with advanced cancer. After long and painful medical treatments, he was so weak that he again thought of quitting. He
_____ that he might never recover from his illness, but once more
(5. knew)
this _____ young man _____ amazing persistence,
(6. energetic) (7. showed)

> **Word level activities** focus on meaning, derivations, grammatical features, and associations.

> Instruction and practice with varying types of word knowledge helps students become **independent word learners**.

Vocabulary Activities STEP II: Sentence Level

The verb *exploit* has the general meaning of "use," but can express two different ideas. It's important to understand which idea is being expressed in a particular sentence.

use something cleverly or productively	*A good student **exploits** every opportunity to read outside of class.*
use something unfairly or selfishly	*Some companies **exploit** workers by not paying them a fair salary.*

The noun form, *exploitation*, almost always has the second, negative meaning.

> *The **exploitation** of workers is unfair.*

CORPUS

E. Work with a partner. Write *P* for the sentences that use *exploit* in a positive way. Write *N* for the sentences that use the word in a negative way.

___ 1. Some parents exploit their children by pushing them to perform in movies or TV shows.

___ 2. He exploited every chance to improve his writing skills.

___ 3. She exploited her friends by borrowing money every day.

___ 4. He exploited his musical talent by playing with a band.

In this unit, *demonstrate* means "to prove or show something." A *demonstrative* person shows his or her feelings very clearly.

> *Her paintings **demonstrate** a great love of her country.*

> *My little granddaughter is so **demonstrative**. She is always hugging me.*

Another common meaning is "to give directions about how something is done."

> *My trainer **demonstrated** how to use the new exercise bicycle.*

To *demonstrate* is also often used to mean "to publicly show your support for or against a social or political cause."

> *A group was **demonstrating** in front of city hall yesterday.*

> *Fifty **demonstrators** took part in a **demonstration** against high taxes.*

CORPUS

> **Vocabulary work progresses** to sentence level and focuses on collocations, register, specific word usage, and learner dictionaries.

From Research to Practice

The Oxford English Corpus provides **the most relevant and accurate picture of the English language**. It is based on a collection of over two billion carefully-selected and inclusive 21st century English texts.

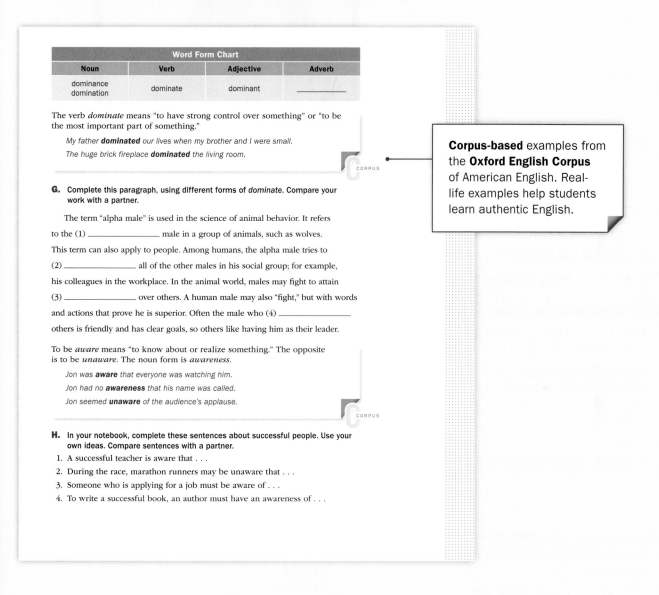

Word Form Chart			
Noun	**Verb**	**Adjective**	**Adverb**
dominance dominasion	dominate	dominant	_____

The verb *dominate* means "to have strong control over something" or "to be the most important part of something."

> *My father* **dominated** *our lives when my brother and I were small.*
> *The huge brick fireplace* **dominated** *the living room.*

CORPUS

G. Complete this paragraph, using different forms of *dominate*. Compare your work with a partner.

The term "alpha male" is used in the science of animal behavior. It refers

to the (1) _____ male in a group of animals, such as wolves.

This term can also apply to people. Among humans, the alpha male tries to

(2) _____ all of the other males in his social group; for example,

his colleagues in the workplace. In the animal world, males may fight to attain

(3) _____ over others. A human male may also "fight," but with words

and actions that prove he is superior. Often the male who (4) _____

others is friendly and has clear goals, so others like having him as their leader.

To be *aware* means "to know about or realize something." The opposite is to be *unaware*. The noun form is *awareness*.

> *Jon was* **aware** *that everyone was watching him.*
> *Jon had no* **awareness** *that his name was called.*
> *Jon seemed* **unaware** *of the audience's applause.*

CORPUS

H. In your notebook, complete these sentences about successful people. Use your own ideas. Compare sentences with a partner.

1. A successful teacher is aware that . . .
2. During the race, marathon runners may be unaware that . . .
3. Someone who is applying for a job must be aware of . . .
4. To write a successful book, an author must have an awareness of . . .

Corpus-based examples from the **Oxford English Corpus** of American English. Real-life examples help students learn authentic English.

Resources

STUDENT SUPPORT

For additional resources visit:
www.oup.com/elt/student/insidereading

> **Reading worksheets** provide additional skill practice
> **Videos** set the stage for specific units
> **Audio recordings** of every reading text

TEACHER SUPPORT

The *Inside Reading* iTools is for use with an LCD projector or interactive whiteboard.

Resources for whole-class presentation
> Audio **recordings** of all **reading texts with "click and listen"** interactive scripts
> **Animated presentations** of reading skills for whole class presentations
> **Videos** for specific units introduce students to the reading text topic and activate prior knowledge.
> **Fun vocabulary activities** for whole-class participation

Resources for assessment and preparation
> Printable worksheets for **extra reading skill practice**
> Printable and customizable **unit, mid-term, and final tests**
> Answer Keys
> Teaching Notes
> Video transcripts

Additional resources at:
www.oup.com/elt/teacher/insidereading

UNIT 1

Riding through History

In this unit, you will

> learn about the changes in technology that led to creating the modern bicycle.
> read about a very different vehicle and how it compares to a bicycle.
> increase your understanding of the target academic words for this unit.

READING SKILL Previewing

Self-Assessment

Think about how well you know each target word, and check (✓) the appropriate column. I have…

TARGET WORDS	never seen the word before	seen the word but am not sure what it means	seen the word and understand what it means	used the word, but am not sure if correctly	used the word confidently in *either* speaking *or* writing	used the word confidently in *both* speaking *and* writing
AWL						
🔑 alter						
🔑 design						
🔑 fee						
framework						
🔑 individual						
inherent						
🔑 injure						
🔑 job						
minimize						
overseas						
🔑 primary						
🔑 revolution						
subsequent						
🔑 substitute						

🔑 Oxford 3000™ keywords

Outside the Reading What do you know about biking?
Watch the video on the student website to find out more.

Before You Read

Read these questions. Discuss your answers in a small group.

1. Do you know how to ride a bicycle? Who taught you to ride? What was the hardest thing to learn?

2. What are some reasons that people ride bicycles?

3. If you could change or improve bicycles, what would you want to do?

READING SKILL Previewing

LEARN

Most good readers spend a few minutes *previewing* before they begin to read. Previewing a book or article means looking it over to get a general idea of what it will be about. It allows you to recall what you already know about a topic, and think about what you are going to learn.

APPLY

Preview Reading 1, below, by answering these questions. Discuss your answers with a partner.

1. Read the summary printed above the article. In a few words, it tells what the article will be about. What do you expect to learn about in the article?

2. Look at the pictures and captions. What information do they give you about the topic?

3. Read the title. You already know that the article will be about bicycles, but what does the word "history" suggest? Read the bold print subheadings at the beginnings of many paragraphs. What information do they give you about the topic? Check (✓) the kind of information that *might* be in the article.

___ when the bicycle was invented

___ a description of the first bicycle

___ changes in the bicycle over time

___ famous bicycle races

___ how to use bicycles for exercise

___ who invented the bicycle

___ how people reacted to the invention

___ how bicycle tires are made

🔊 **Read**

This article from a popular technology magazine tells about the many changes in bicycles during the past 200 years.

The History of Bicycles

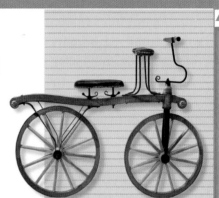

The bicycle was not invented by one **individual** or in one country. The creation of the modern bicycle took nearly 100 years and the work of many **individuals**. By the end of those 100 years,
5 bicycles had **revolutionized** the way people traveled from place to place.

EARLY BICYCLES

Bicycles first appeared in Scotland in the early 1800s, and were called velocipedes. These early bicycles had two wheels, but they had no pedals. A rider sat on a pillow and walked his feet along the
10 ground to move his velocipede forward.

Soon a French inventor added pedals to the front wheel. Instead of walking their vehicles, riders used their feet to turn the pedals. However, pedaling was hard because velocipedes were very heavy. The **frameworks** were made of solid steel tubes, and the wooden
15 wheels were covered with steel. Even so, velocipedes were popular among rich young men, who raced them in Paris parks.

Because velocipedes were so hard to ride, no one thought about using them for transportation. People didn't ride velocipedes to the market or to their **jobs**. Instead, people thought velocipedes were just toys.

SOME CHANGES ARE MADE

20 Around 1870, American manufacturers saw that velocipedes were very popular **overseas.** They began building velocipedes, too, but with one difference. They made the **frameworks** from hollow steel tubes. This **alteration** made velocipedes much lighter, but riders still had to work hard to pedal just a short distance. In addition,
25 roads were bumpy, so steering was difficult. In fact, most riders preferred indoor tracks where they could rent a velocipede for a small **fee** and take riding lessons.

THE HIGH WHEELER

A **subsequent** change by British engineers **altered** the wheels to make pedaling more efficient. They saw that when a rider turned

30 the pedals once, the front wheel turned once. If the front wheel was small, the bicycle traveled just a small distance with each turn. They reasoned that if the front wheel were larger, the bicycle would travel a greater distance with each

35 turn of the pedals. So they **designed** a bicycle with a giant front wheel. They made the rear wheel small. Its **primary** purpose was to help the rider balance. Balancing was hard because riders had to sit high above the giant front wheel in

40 order to reach the pedals. This meant they were in danger of falling off the bicycle and **injuring** themselves if they lost their balance. Despite this **inherent** danger, "high wheelers" became very popular in England.

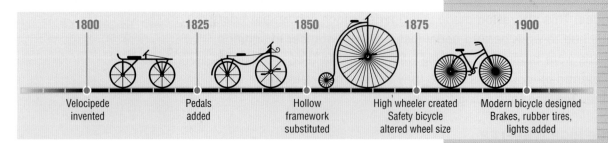

A SAFER BICYCLE

American manufacturers once again tried to **design** a better

45 bicycle. Their goal was to make a safer bicycle. They **substituted** a small wheel for the giant front wheel and put the driving mechanism in a larger rear wheel. It would be impossible for a rider to pedal the rear wheel, so engineers **designed** a system of foot levers. By pressing first the right one and then the left, the

50 rider moved a long metal bar up and down. This turned the rear wheel, and the bicycle moved forward. Because the new safety bicycle **minimized** the dangers **inherent** in bicycle riding, more and more people began using bicycles in their daily activities.

THE MODERN BICYCLE IS BORN

The British **altered** the **design** one last time. They made the two

55 wheels equal in size and created a mechanism that used a chain to turn the rear wheel. With this final change the modern bicycle was born.

Subsequent improvements, such as brakes, rubber tires, and lights, were added to make bicycles more comfortable to ride. By 1900, bicycle riding had become very popular with men and

60 women of all ages. Bicycles **revolutionized** the way people traveled. Today, millions of people worldwide ride bicycles for transportation, enjoyment, sport, and exercise.

1800	1825	1850	1875	1900
Velocipede invented	Pedals added	Hollow framework substituted	High wheeler created Safety bicycle altered wheel size	Modern bicycle designed Brakes, rubber tires, lights added

Reading Comprehension

Mark each statement as *T* (True) or *F* (False) according to the information in Reading 1. Use your dictionary to check the meaning of new words.

___ 1. Many individuals took part in creating the modern bicycle.

___ 2. The first bicycle revolutionized travel in Scotland and overseas.

___ 3. Early velocipedes had frameworks made of solid steel tubes.

___ 4. American manufacturers substituted hollow steel tubes for the solid tubes.

___ 5. People in Paris paid a fee to ride velocipedes to their jobs.

___ 6. The primary purpose of the giant front wheel was to help the rider balance.

___ 7. American manufacturers designed a bicycle with a small rear wheel that was inherently safer.

___ 8. The modern bicycle was born when British engineers subsequently altered the wheels again and made them equal in size.

Vocabulary Activities   STEP I: Word Level

A. Read this passage about the Tour de France, a world-famous bicycle race. In each sentence, circle the one word or phrase in parentheses ( ) that has the same meaning as the underlined word in the sentence. Compare your answers with a partner. Then take turns reading the sentences to each other using the circled words.

1. The course for the Tour de France is <u>altered</u> (*measured /* *changed /* *marked*) every year, but it is always about 4,000 kilometers, or 2,500 miles.

2. The course is <u>designed</u> (*located / expected / planned*) to travel through towns, up steep mountains, and across flat lands.

3. Riders come from all over Europe as well as from <u>overseas</u> (*islands / abroad / oceans*) to take part in the 22-day race.

4. The race is divided into 20 stages, or parts. The rider who wins one stage has the honor of wearing a yellow Tour shirt in the <u>subsequent</u> (*final / longest / next*) stage.

5. The rider who has the fastest race time in all of the stages is the overall winner. Lance Armstrong is the only <u>individual</u> (*person / man / foreigner*) to win seven Tour de France competitions.

6. The <u>framework</u> (*mechanism / structure / wheel*) of modern racing bicycles is made of lightweight steel, aluminum, titanium, and carbon fiber tubes.

7. The recent use of lightweight frameworks brought about <u>revolutionary</u> (*unwanted / unfair / great*) changes in the 100-year-old race.

8. Teams pay an entrance <u>fee</u> (*payment / tax / salary*) to join the Tour de France. The fees create the prize money paid to the winning teams.

9. Riders must be good athletes to meet the physical demands that are an <u>inherent</u> (*unexpected / natural / dangerous*) part of a long race.

10. If a rider is <u>injured</u> (*sick / tired / hurt*), he tries to <u>minimize</u> (*lessen / hide / endure*) the pain so he can stay in the race.

11. If the pain is too bad, the coach can assign a teammate to <u>substitute for</u> (*help* / *take out* / *replace*) the injured rider.

12. The <u>primary</u> (*main* / *total* / *easiest*) <u>job</u> (*purpose* / *employment* / *skill*) of a Tour coach is to help his team win.

B. To *minimize* something is to make it less or to reduce its importance. Think about the problems that racing cyclists can have. With a partner, match the problem on the right with the item that can minimize it on the left. Then take turns creating sentences with the information.

a 1. knee braces   a. stress on knees

  *Knee braces can **minimize** stress on knees.*

___ 2. low handle bars   b. thirst

___ 3. a helmet   c. sunburn

___ 4. long sleeves   d. sprains

___ 5. water   e. head injuries

___ 6. ice   f. air drag

The adjective *inherent* refers to a natural, built-in quality of a person, object, or activity. *Inherently* is the adverb form.

  Staying balanced is an **inherent** challenge for bicycle riders.

  Bicycle racing is **inherently** dangerous.

CORPUS

C. With a partner, check (✓) the sports you think are inherently dangerous. Add one more. Then discuss the reasons for your choices in a small group.

___ snow skiing   ___ race-car driving

___ golf   ___ horseback riding

___ soccer   ___ motorcycle racing

___ basketball   ___ swimming

___ long-distance running   ___ mountain climbing

___ tennis   ___ other: _____

Primary refers to something that is first, main, or basic. Here are some examples of collocations (words that go together) using the word *primary:*

  primary colors primary elections

  primary school primary care physician

CORPUS

D. With a partner, match the worker on the left with his or her primary job on the right. Take turns creating sentences with the information.

a 1. tailor   a. altering clothing to fit individuals

  *A tailor's **primary** job is altering clothing to fit individuals.*

___ 2. architect   b. teaching the classes of a teacher who is absent

___ 3. taxi driver   c. driving people from place to place for a fee

___ 4. international airline pilot   d. designing buildings

___ 5. doctor   e. cleaning and taking care of buildings

___ 6. substitute teacher   f. helping individuals who are injured or sick

___ 7. janitor   g. flying airplanes overseas

Which of the workers in activity D do their jobs primarily during the day? Which of the workers might also work at night?

Vocabulary Activities   STEP II: Sentence Level

Word Form Chart			
Noun	**Verb**	**Adjective**	**Adverb**
revolution	revolutionize	revolutionary	_____

The central meaning of *revolution* is "turning" or "changing." It can refer to one thing rotating around a central point, like the Earth's revolution around the sun. It can also mean "changing or trying to change the political system by violent action."

In this unit, *revolution* is used to mean "a complete change in methods, opinions, etc., often as a result of progress."

> Bicycles led to a **revolution** in transportation.
>
> Bicycles **revolutionized** the way people traveled from place to place.
>
> Bicycles were a **revolutionary** idea.

CORPUS

E. **In your notebook, rewrite these sentences two ways. Use a different form of *revolution* in each sentence.**

1. The addition of sound changed the way motion pictures told stories. (noun, verb)

   *The sound **revolution** changed the way motion pictures told stories. (noun)*

   *The addition of sound **revolutionized** the way motion pictures told a story. (verb)*

2. The jet engine caused a change in air travel. (verb, adj.)

3. Alfred Nobel created a new substance that he called "dynamite." (noun, adj.)

4. The discovery of X-rays changed medical science. (noun, adj.)

The verb *substitute* means to replace one thing for something different.
The noun form *substitution* refers to the process of making a replacement.
The noun form *substitute* refers to the person or thing that will be used to replace something.

> The team captain **substituted** Ernesto for the injured player.
>
> He made the **substitution** because the injured player was in pain.
>
> The **substitute** went on to win the game.

The word *substitute* is commonly used for a teacher or player who takes someone else's place.

> We had a **substitute** in math class today.

 CORPUS

F. Make words related to bicycles. Remove one letter from each word and substitute the given letter to make a new word. Tell a partner how to make the new words.

1. chair/n   *Substitute an N for the R to make chain.* _____
2. steel/r: _____
3. time/r _____
4. broke/a _____
5. hide/r _____
6. petal/d _____

Subsequent is an adjective that refers to something that is later than or follows something else. The adverb form is *subsequently*.

> Henry Ford's first car was called the Model T. The **subsequent** Model A was introduced in 1927.
>
> Henry Ford created the Model T in 1908. **Subsequently**, he built the Model A.

CORPUS

G. Complete each sentence with forms of *subsequent* AND *substitute*. Be sure to use the correct form of each word.

1. The wheels of the first velocipedes had no pedals, but a French inventor _____ _____ wheels that had pedals.

2. European velocipedes were heavy because the framework was made of solid steel tubes. The _____ _____ of hollow steel tubes by American manufacturers made the vehicles much lighter.

3. The high wheeler had a small rear wheel. A _____ change by American manufacturers _____ the larger rear wheel for the smaller one.

Before You Read

Read these questions. Discuss your answers in a small group.

1. How much do you walk in your daily activities? Do you sometimes wish you could walk less? When?

2. How do you decide if you should walk, ride a bicycle, or drive when you go somewhere?

3. Have you ever seen a Segway? Describe where you saw it and what it looked like.

READING SKILL | Previewing

APPLY

Preview Reading 2 by answering these questions. Discuss your answers with a partner.

1. Look at the title of the article. Does the title tell you what it will be about? What does the word *future* in the title suggest about the article? How do you think this article will be different from the previous reading in this unit?

2. Look at the picture in the article. Does it help explain what a Segway is?

3. Read the bold type subheadings. What information do they give about the topic? Check (✓) the questions that *might* be answered in the article.

___ Where are Segways used?

___ Who will ride Segways?

___ How are they like bicycles?

___ When was the Segway invented?

___ Where is the engine?

___ How much do they cost?

___ What are they used for?

___ How many Segways are there in Paris?

This newspaper article poses questions about the future of personal transport.

Segway Into the Future

For nearly two hundred years, **individuals** worldwide have been riding bicycles for transportation, enjoyment, sport, and exercise. In 2001, the Segway, a **revolutionary**
5 new vehicle, was introduced. The inventor imagined that the Segway might someday replace bicycles. Would this be possible? How does a Segway compare to a bicycle?

WHAT IS A SEGWAY?

Both Segways and bicycles are **designed** to carry
10 one rider. However, Segway riders do not sit on a seat. Instead, they stand on a platform while they are riding. The platform is the floor of a strong metal **framework**. A post with handles for the rider to hold is attached to the front of the
15 platform. A wide rubber wheel is attached to each side of the platform. Except for these two wheels, there are no mechanical parts on a Segway. Like a bicycle, it has no engine. However, unlike a bicycle, a Segway has no brakes, no pedals, no
20 gears, and no steering mechanism.

Control post

Handles

Platform

Wheels

HOW A SEGWAY MOVES

A Segway uses a computer system that is **designed** to respond to the **inherent** ability of riders to maintain their balance. For example, without thinking about it, a rider actually leans his body slightly forward when he expects to move forward. When the rider expects to stop, he leans his body
25 slightly back. When the rider thinks about moving left or right, he leans left or right. The computer system checks the rider's body movements about 100 times every second. Instantly, the Segway moves forward, stops, or turns in response to every slight change in the rider's balance. It is easy to learn to ride a Segway because it responds to the rider's natural movements.

HOW A BICYCLE MOVES

30 In contrast, it is hard to learn to ride a bicycle. The rider works constantly to stay balanced. She turns the pedals with her feet to make the bicycle move forward. She presses the brake levers to make the bicycle stop. To

alter her direction, the rider moves the handle bars left or right. If a bicycle rider leans too far to one side, the bicycle will **subsequently** fall over.

Riding a bicycle is also hard work. A bicycle can travel as far as a rider can keep pedaling. It can go very fast if the rider has enough energy to pedal hard. For example, in the annual Tour de France bicycle race, riders travel more than 100 miles a day at speeds greater than 30 miles per hour.

A Segway race would not be very interesting. A Segway can't go very far, and it can't go very fast. A Segway is powered by a battery that limits it to traveling 24 miles (39 kilometers) on one battery charge. And it can travel no faster than 12.5 miles (20 kilometers) per hour. Being battery-powered, not pedal-powered, the rider gets almost no exercise, but Segways are fun. **Overseas** and at home, they are popular with tourists. Visitors to over 200 cities, including London, Athens, and Bangkok, can pay a **fee** to take a guided city tour on a Segway.

BICYCLES AND SEGWAYS COMPARED		
	Bicycles	**Segways**
Riders	One	One
Power	Pedaling	Battery
Top speed	30+ mph	12.5 mph
Range	Unlimited	24 miles per battery charge
Indoors/Outdoors	Outdoors	Indoors and outdoors
Easy to learn	No	Yes
Easy to balance	No	Yes
Provides exercise	Yes	No
Provides transportation	Yes	Limited

HOW SEGWAYS ARE USED

Segways can do things that bicycles cannot do. For instance, Segways are useful in **jobs** that normally require workers to do a lot of walking, such as delivering mail, inspecting farms, or patrolling buildings at night. An extra benefit is that **individuals** who cannot comfortably walk because of poor health or **injury** can **minimize** their walking but still be able to work if they can ride a Segway.

Segways are useful in other kinds of **jobs,** too. Pizza restaurants, pharmacies, and other small businesses have **substituted** Segways for trucks to make neighborhood deliveries. Police departments around the world have been putting officers on Segways instead of in cars or on motorcycles. The officers can patrol neighborhoods to keep them safe from crime. In many countries, security guards on Segways patrol airports, train stations, amusement parks, and other public places. Beijing public safety police patrolled on Segways during the 2008 Olympics.

WHY SEGWAYS ARE NOT USED MORE

65 However, few people are buying Segways for their own use. One reason may be that they are expensive. Another may be that people fear being laughed at for buying a "toy." A **primary** reason, however, may be that people do not understand what a Segway is, and they are afraid that it is dangerous. Some cities have even passed laws that allow Segways to travel
70 only on sidewalks. The cities are concerned that Segway riders will cause accidents if they ride in the streets. Other cities allow Segways only in street bicycle lanes. They are concerned that people on the sidewalk might be **injured** by a Segway. Meanwhile, many cities are creating new bicycle paths and street traffic lanes to encourage people to ride bicycles.
75 Will Segways ever replace bicycles? Probably not, but they can do certain **jobs** that bicycles cannot do. Segways are hard-working vehicles that we are likely to see more of in the future. ■

Reading Comprehension

Mark each statement as *T* (True) or *F* (False) according to the information in Reading 2. Use your dictionary to check the meaning of new words.

___ 1. The Segway's framework consists of a platform and a post with handles.

___ 2. The driver can alter the direction of the Segway by leaning to the left or right.

___ 3. The Segway was primarily designed for individuals who cannot walk comfortably.

___ 4. Workers have been injured while riding Segways on their jobs.

___ 5. If the driver leans forward, the Segway subsequently slows down.

___ 6. People seem to have an inherent fear of electric vehicles.

___ 7. For a fee, people can take a tour on a Segway in some cities overseas.

___ 8. Segways can substitute for trucks to make neighborhood deliveries.

___ 9. Segways can minimize the walking that some jobs require.

Vocabulary Activities   STEP I: Word Level

A. Use the target vocabulary in the box to complete this story. Use the words in parentheses to help you.

alter	individual	an inherent	revolutionized
designed	injured	minimize	subsequent
framework	had a job	primary	substituted

In 1901, Glenn Curtiss was 23 years old and _____ (1. worked at) manufacturing and selling bicycles. He had _____ (2. a natural) love of speed. He wanted to find a way to _____ (3. change) bicycles so they could go faster than a rider could pedal them. Glenn _____ (4. made the plans for) an engine that

_____ a tomato can for a carburetor. He attached the engine to the
(5. replaced)

drive mechanism of a bicycle. However, the engine did not make the bicycle go

much faster, despite the loud noise it made. A _____ engine that
(6. later)

Glenn built was too heavy, and the bicycle was hard to balance. Riders often tipped

over and _____ themselves. The heavy weight of the engine was the
(7. hurt)

_____ problem he had to solve. After many tries to
(8. main)

_____ the weight, he solved the problem by making the
(9. lessen)

_____ stronger. He began racing his "motorcycle." In 1907, Glenn set
(10. structure)

a speed record. He went 136 miles per hour, faster than any _____ in
(11. person)

the world had ever traveled. Glenn's invention _____ bicycle riding.
(12. created a big change in)

A word analogy shows the relationship between two sets of words. To solve
an analogy, you must identify how the words in the first set are related. Here
are some examples.

apple : fruit	example	An *apple* is an example of a *fruit*.
pretty : lovely	synonym	*Pretty* and *lovely* have similar meanings.
young : old	antonym	*Young* and *old* have opposite meanings.
bicycle : ride	action	*Ride* is the action when you use a *bicycle*.
room : house	part	A *room* is part of a *house*.

To finish an analogy, think of a word to complete the second set of words
that has the same relationship as the first set.

　　apple : fruit AS carrot : _____

An apple is an example of a fruit, so the missing word is *vegetable*. *Carrot* is
an example of a *vegetable*.

You say an analogy like this: "*Apple* is to *fruit* as *carrot* is to *vegetable*."

CORPUS

B. With a partner, use the target vocabulary in the box to complete these analogies.
Then write the type of relationship each analogy has.

　　　　　　　　　　　　　　　　　　　　　　　　　　　　　Relationship

1. garden : flower AS crowd : ___*individual*___　　　___*part*___

2. car : damage AS person : _____　　　_____

3. save : spend AS increase : _____　　　_____

4. nation : country AS abroad : _____　　　_____

5. write : check AS pay : _____　　　_____

6. false : true AS last : _____　　　_____

7. bus : vehicle AS bus driver : _____　　　_____

8. before : after AS earlier : _____　　　_____

C. With a partner, decide if these lines from advertisements were written before 1900 to sell early bicycles or after 2001 to sell modern Segways. Mark an advertisement *B* for bicycles or *S* for Segways.

___ Hollow steel tubes substituted for solid tubes to minimize the weight.

___ Lean forward and watch this revolutionary vehicle go!

___ Individuals can alter their speed by just turning the pedals.

___ Used overseas to patrol the Beijing Olympics.

___ Avoid injuries. For a small fee, learn to ride on an indoor track.

___ Inherently easy to drive. Primary power is from batteries.

___ You thought high-wheelers were great? Try the subsequent design!

A *framework* is a structure upon which other parts are built or attached. On a bicycle, the wheels, pedals, and handlebars are attached to the steel framework. Sometimes, *framework* refers to the basis or foundation of something.

> The **frameworks** of early velocipedes were made of solid steel tubes.
>
> A good education forms the **framework** for a successful career.

CORPUS

D. With a partner, match the frameworks on the right with the object or system that they support on the left. Take turns making sentences with the information.

> The **framework** of a human body is the skeleton.

___ 1. a human body   a. steel beams

___ 2. many governments   b. an interesting plot

___ 3. a skyscraper   c. the number 10

___ 4. the metric system   d. a constitution

___ 5. a good book   e. the skeleton

To *alter* something means "to make something different in some way, but without changing it completely." If you alter something, you have made an *alteration*.

Some things that you might alter include items of clothing, plans, or opinions.

CORPUS

E. With a partner, imagine that you have borrowed a friend's bicycle for the weekend. Which things can be altered on a borrowed bicycle? Write *A* for each item you could alter.

___ the speed of the bicycle   ___ the size of the wheels

___ the color of the framework   ___ the direction the bicycle turns

___ the height of the seat   ___ the speed that the wheels turn

___ the design of the bicycle   ___ the mirrors on the handlebars

Word Form Chart			
Noun	**Verb**	**Adjective**	**Adverb**
design designer	design	designed	_____
individual individuality	individualize	individual individualized	individually

The noun *individual* means "person." The plural is *individuals*.

*There were 200 **individuals** in the research study.*

The adjective *individual* means something intended for one person.

*Each bowl contained an **individual** serving of rice.*

Individually means to perform an action one person or object at a time.

*She washed each glass **individually**.*

To *individualize* something means to make it special for each person.

*The teacher **individualized** the assignment by giving each student a different topic to write about. We had **individualized** topics.*

Individuality refers to what makes a person unlike any other person.

*Twins may show their **individuality** by wearing different clothing.*

CORPUS

F. The Pinewood Derby is a car race sponsored by the Boy Scouts of America. The cars are small—just seven inches long. Rewrite these sentences about the Pinewood Derby to include the word in parentheses. Discuss your sentences with a partner.

1. Each boy works by himself to make his own cars. (*individually*)

2. First each boy makes a plan of his car on paper. (*design*, verb)

3. He wants to make his car look like no other cars in the derby, so it will be special. (*individualize*)

4. He can show his unique personality in many ways. Some boys plan their cars to look like a snake or a hot dog, for example. (*individuality, design*)

5. To build the car, the creator traces his plan on a block of wood and carves out the shape. Then he attaches the wheels and paints his car. (*designer, design*)

6. On the day of the race, the Boy Scouts roll their cars down a sloped board one at a time. The fastest car down the board wins a prize. (*individually*)

7. The judges give separate prizes for the funniest car, the scariest car, and other categories. (*individual*, adj.)

8. Every car is a winner. The contest is planned to show every boy's special qualities. (*designed*, verb; *individuality*)

G. In your notebook, rewrite each of these sentences to include the words in parentheses ( ). Share your sentences with a partner or small group.

1. Great changes in transportation have taken place in the last 200 years. (*revolutionary*)

   Revolutionary changes in transportation have taken place in the last 200 years.

2. Farmers replaced animals with tractors to pull their plows. (*substituted for*)

3. Airplanes made traveling across oceans easier and faster. (*overseas*)

4. Jet airplanes made the time of flights shorter. (*minimized*)

5. No one walks anymore. People travel mostly on wheels. (*primarily*)

6. The first airplane was made of wood covered by cloth. (*framework*)

7. Segways rely on the natural ability of riders to maintain their balance. (*inherent*)

8. Early trains were powered by steam. Then changes were made in their plans so they could be powered by diesel engines. (*subsequent/alterations/designs*)

H. Self-Assessment Review: Go back to page 1 and reassess your knowledge of the target vocabulary. How has your understanding of the words changed? What words do you feel most comfortable with now?

Writing and Discussion Topics

With a partner or small group, share ideas about the following topics. Then have each person write a paragraph about one of the topics.

1. Imagine that you work as a police officer in a small city. Your department has purchased a Segway for each officer who patrols the city streets. Yesterday was your first day patrolling on your Segway. Use your imagination and write a story about how you used the Segway, what you liked, and what problems you had.

2. Reading 1 ends with, "Today, millions of people worldwide ride bicycles for transportation, enjoyment, sport, and exercise." Describe examples of each of these uses.

3. The Segway was not designed to be used for sport; however, some people believe that certain team sports could be adapted for players riding Segways. What sports could be adapted to use Segways? How would the players in each sport use them?

Fighting Diseases

In this unit, you will

> read about the causes and effects of malaria in sub-Saharan Africa.
> read about sources of new medicines.
> review previewing a reading text.
> increase your understanding of the target academic words for this unit.

READING SKILL Finding the Main Idea

Self-Assessment

Think about how well you know each target word, and check (✓) the appropriate column. I have…

TARGET WORDS	never seen the word before	seen the word but am not sure what it means	seen the word and understand what it means	used the word, but am not sure if correctly	used the word confidently in *either* speaking *or* writing	used the word confidently in *both* speaking *and* writing
AWL						
🔑 access						
🔑 accompany						
🔑 conflict						
cooperate						
🔑 decline						
implement						
🔑 intense						
🔑 labor						
🔑 medical						
🔑 ministry						
🔑 occur						
practitioner						
🔑 priority						
reside						

🔑 Oxford 3000™ keywords

 Outside the Reading What do you know about medicine?
Watch the video on the student website to find out more.

Before You Read

Read these questions. Discuss your answers in a small group.

1. Have you ever been very sick? What did you do to get well? How long did it take to get well?

2. What are some ways to prevent an illness?

3. Do you know of any insects that are helpful to humans? How do they help? Do you know of any insects that are harmful to humans? How are they harmful?

REVIEW A SKILL Previewing (See p. 2)

Preview Reading 1. Look at the title and the bold subtitles in the article. Look at the photos. What do these things tell you about the article? What do you expect to learn from the article?

Read

This journal article includes information from the website of the Centers for Disease Control and Prevention (CDC), the principal public health agency in the United States.

THE BATTLE AGAINST MALARIA

Malaria is a serious health problem. It is a leading cause of death in many countries. It **occurs** mostly in tropical and subtropical parts of the world, including parts of Africa, Asia, South America, Central America, and the Middle East. The place most **intensely** affected by malaria

5 is Africa south of the Sahara Desert. About 60% of the world's malaria cases and 90% of malaria deaths **occur** there. Even though the causes of malaria in this region are well understood, international health agencies are finding that controlling it is still an enormous and difficult task.

THE MALARIA CYCLE

Malaria is passed from mosquitoes to people and from

10 people to mosquitoes in a cycle of events that repeats over and over. The malaria cycle begins with tiny parasites. These parasites **reside** in the bodies of *Anopheles* mosquitoes. These deadly parasites cause malaria. When a female mosquito bites a human, the mosquito draws off

15 blood. It also leaves malaria parasites in the human's skin.

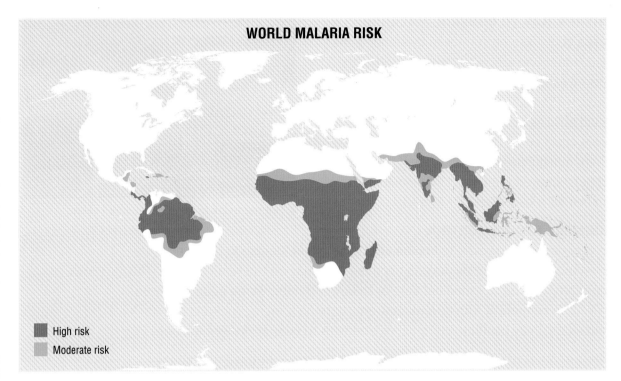

WORLD MALARIA RISK

High risk
Moderate risk

These parasites quickly multiply inside the human and cause the individual to feel sick. If another mosquito bites a human who is sick with malaria, parasites from the human enter the body of the mosquito. When that mosquito bites another human, it will leave parasites in the other human's skin. In the malaria
20 cycle, humans get parasites from mosquitoes and humans also give parasites to mosquitoes.

EMERGENCY MEDICAL CARE NEEDED

Becoming infected with malaria is a **medical** emergency. The first symptoms—or signs—of malaria are fever, chills, sweating, **intense** headache, and muscle pains. Nausea and vomiting often **accompany** these symptoms. Immediate
25 **medical** treatment must be a **priority** for people who are infected. They must take medicines that will kill the parasites. If **medical** treatment is started soon enough, sick individuals can be cured. If it is not, malaria can cause serious illness or even death.

ONE WAY TO CONTROL MALARIA

Malaria in tropical Africa could be controlled in two ways. First, it could be
30 controlled by killing the parasites that cause the illness. If every infected person quickly took malaria medicine, most would be well in a few days. Mosquitoes could not get malaria parasites from healthy individuals, so malaria would not spread. Unfortunately, many people live in far-away villages without **access** to quick **medical** care. Another problem is that the ability of quinine
35 (the primary medicine used against malaria) to kill parasites has **declined** over time. There is hope, however, for new drug combinations. One, called ACT, is being used successfully to treat people who have malaria.

ANOTHER WAY TO CONTROL MALARIA

Malaria could also be controlled by stopping the
40 mosquitoes. One way would be to get rid of the
pools of water where they lay their eggs. Also,
insecticide¹ could be sprayed in wet areas and
around buildings to kill mosquitoes. Finally,
people could be told to sleep under bed nets to
45 prevent mosquitoes from biting them at night.
Bed nets sprayed with insecticide would both
stop and kill mosquitoes.

A bed net helps to keep mosquitoes away.

PROBLEMS FACING CONTROL

It is very difficult, however, to **implement** these plans. People in this region are
poor—and made poorer by malaria because they may be too weak to work. They
50 cannot afford to pay for **medical** care or to buy bed nets. Some people may be
unwilling to **cooperate** with government efforts to help them. Their old beliefs
about illness may **conflict** with modern attempts to cure or prevent malaria.

There are other problems, too. Health **ministries** may not have the money to
build clinics or hire trained **medical practitioners**. They may not have the
55 money to buy insect poisons and pay a **labor** force to spray regularly. And the
frequent rainfall in tropical and subtropical regions would make it impossible to
get rid of pools of water where mosquitoes lay eggs.

A recent discovery by **medical** scientists may offer a solution to many of these
problems. In 2009, the **Ministry** of Health in Senegal arranged for scientists to
60 visit three villages. A tropical illness called "river blindness" was common in these
villages. The people were given the medicine ivermectin to treat it. Two weeks after
the people had taken the medicine, the scientists found many dead mosquitoes.
They discovered that when a mosquito bit a person who had recently taken
ivermectin, the mosquito died. It was poisoned by the medicine in the person's
65 blood. Now scientists wonder if malaria could be controlled by **implementing** a
program to give this medicine to people every month. They need to find out if
taking *ivermectin* every month will be safe. They also are waiting to see if there will
be a **decline** in malaria cases in these villages. If it is safe and effective, this
medicine could help stop the spread of malaria in sub-Saharan Africa.

---

¹ *insecticide:* a poison that kills insects

Reading Comprehension

**Mark each statement as *T* (True) or *F* (False) according to the information in
Reading 1. Use your dictionary to check the meaning of new words.**

____ 1. Malaria occurs mostly in tropical and subtropical parts of the world.

____ 2. Deadly malaria parasites reside in the bodies of mosquitoes.

____ 3. Intense coughing and sneezing often accompany the fever of malaria.

____ 4. Old beliefs may conflict with modern ways to cure or prevent illness.

____ 5. Getting fast medical attention after becoming ill is a priority.

____ 6. Sleeping under bed nets would lead to a decline in malaria.

___ 7. Health ministries in some countries often cannot afford to implement plans to control malaria.

___ 8. Most people in tropical Africa have easy access to medical practitioners.

___ 9. Educated people are not willing to cooperate with government plans to help them.

___10. A large labor force would be needed to spray insecticide regularly.

READING SKILL | Finding the Main Idea

LEARN

The *topic* of an article refers to what the article is about. The *main idea* of an article goes one step further. The main idea includes the topic and also what the writer wants to say about the topic. For example:

Topic	Main idea
malaria	*several ways to control malaria*

The main idea of an article is usually stated in the first paragraph, often in the first or last sentence. Sometimes it is stated in the last paragraph, which often summarizes the article. The main idea may be a full sentence or just a few words.

Each paragraph in an article contributes its own facts, definitions, and examples that help explain the main idea of the article. This means that each paragraph has its own main idea. Often it is in the first sentence of the paragraph.

APPLY

Reread the first paragraph of Reading 1. Find the sentence that tells you the *main idea*—what the writer wants to say about malaria—and circle it. Then write the most important part of the sentence here, as the main idea.

_____

_____

Reread the paragraphs below. Find the sentence that includes the main idea. Compare the main idea to the three choices (a, b, or c). Circle the one that best states the main idea.

PARAGRAPH 2

a. The malaria cycle begins with tiny parasites.
b. *Anopheles* mosquitoes are deadly.
c. Parasites quickly multiply.

PARAGRAPH 4

a. Malaria can cause death.
b. Becoming infected is a medical emergency.
c. Sick people must take medicine.

PARAGRAPH 7

a. The people of the region need education about malaria.
b. Plans to prevent malaria are difficult to implement.
c. Malaria makes people poorer because they cannot work.

A. *Practitioner* is a formal word to describe someone who practices a specific profession. With a partner, match these practitioners with their descriptions.

___ 1. a practitioner of law   a. a nurse who has had extra training and can perform some services of a doctor

___ 2. a nurse-practitioner   b. someone who teaches others

___ 3. a practitioner of sports   c. someone licensed to represent someone else in legal matters

___ 4. a practitioner of education   d. an athlete

A *ministry* is a governmental department that oversees the administration of one area of responsibility. A ministry is headed by a *minister*. He or she is in charge of the *ministerial* duties of the department. The head of a government is often called the *prime minister*.

Not all countries use these titles, however. The governments of Mexico and the United States, for example, have *departments* headed by *secretaries*. The head of the government is called the *president*.

CORPUS

B. With a partner, match each government ministry to its area of responsibility. Take turns making sentences with the information.

*The **Ministry** of Finance is responsible for the national budget.*

_a_ 1. Ministry of Finance   a. the national budget

___ 2. Ministry of Health   b. working conditions in factories

___ 3. Ministry of Labor   c. airlines and trains

___ 4. Ministry of Agriculture   d. hospitals and healthcare practitioners

___ 5. Ministry of Transportation   e. farm products

Now, tell your partner the title of the person in charge of each ministry.

*The **Minister** of Finance is in charge of the Ministry of Finance.*

C. With a partner, decide which of these conditions should be treated medically. Check (✓) your answers.

___ 1. a broken arm   ___ 4. an earache   ___ 7. choking

___ 2. hair loss   ___ 5. a heart attack   ___ 8. sneezing

___ 3. a broken fingernail   ___ 6. a high fever   ___ 9. an eye injury

A *conflict* (noun, pronounced CON-flict) is a disagreement or a difference in ideas or plans. It can be serious or not, depending on the context.

> Two nations had an armed **conflict** that lasted five years.
> Ms. Ellis had a scheduling **conflict**. She had two meetings at 9 a.m.

To *conflict* (verb, pronounced con-FLICT) means "to happen at the same time" or "to be in disagreement." The adjective form is *conflicting*.

> Her staff meeting **conflicts** with a sales meeting.
> Two professors had **conflicting** ideas about history.

CORPUS

D. Which of these pairs of newspaper headlines have conflicting information? Discuss with a partner why they conflict or don't conflict.

1. a. HEALTH MINISTRY REPORTS A DECLINE IN MALARIA
   b. MALARIA NUMBERS INCREASE THIS YEAR

2. a. GOVERNMENT IMPLEMENTS NEW HEALTH PROGRAM
   b. NEW HEALTH PROGRAM PUT INTO SERVICE

3. a. STAFF TO ACCOMPANY PRIME MINISTER ON OVERSEAS TRIP
   b. PRIME MINISTER TO GO OVERSEAS ALONE

E. The noun *labor* refers to hard or difficult work. The verb is also *labor*. With a partner, discuss what these people might be doing when they are laboring. Which people are probably paid for their labor? Which ones probably receive no money for their labor?

1. a student
2. a farmer
3. an auto mechanic
4. a cook
5. a housewife
6. a poet
7. a musician
8. a gardener

Vocabulary Activities STEP II: Sentence Level

Word Form Chart			
Noun	**Verb**	**Adjective**	**Adverb**
intensity intensification	intensify	intense intensive	intensely intensively

The adjective *intense* refers to something that is strong or extreme. Something *intensive* suggests a strong focus of effort, power, etc. The verb *intensify* means to increase in strength. Other forms of *intense* have related meanings.

> People have developed an **intense** fear of malaria.
>
> Doctors have **intensified** their efforts to control the disease.
>
> They have started an **intensive** program to educate people.

Some common collocations: intense fear/anger/hunger/headache/odor/light, intensive program/care/study/effort/therapy

CORPUS

F. Rewrite these sentences to include a form of *intense*.

1. The common cold often causes strong feelings in schools.

   *Students who have a cold often cause **intense** feelings in the classroom.*

2. Teachers strongly dislike having sick children in their classes.

3. They say that children with severe coughs belong at home.

4. A sick child in class strengthens the chances that other children will get sick.

5. Our school's strong health program urges students to stay home if they are sick.

The *priority* of something refers to its importance or value in relation to other things. It is usually accompanied by an adjective.

> *My children are my <u>highest</u> **priority** in life.*

> *Hospitals give patients with minor injuries the <u>lowest</u> **priority**.*

When no adjective accompanies the word, it means simply *important*. If something is not important, it is not a priority.

> *Time is a **priority** here.*   *In this situation, time is important.*

> *Color is not a **priority**.*   *Color is not important in this situation.*

To prioritize things (goals, tasks, etc.) means to list or do them in the order of importance.

G. Imagine that you work with the international organization Doctors Without Borders. Your team has just arrived in a country where most of the people are sick with malaria. With a partner, prioritize these actions—that is, rank them for importance. Write *1* for the highest priority, *2* for the next highest, etc. Give reasons for your prioritization.

___ spraying homes with insecticide   ___ giving food to sick people

___ cutting down tall grass   ___ getting rid of pools of water

___ giving medicine to sick people   ___ teaching people to wash their hands

Word Form Chart			
Noun	**Verb**	**Adjective**	**Adverb**
resident residence resides residences (people) (places)	reside	residential	residentially

To *reside* somewhere is to live somewhere or make your home somewhere. A *resident* is a person who lives in a particular place. The plural is *residents*. The place where a person lives is his or her *residence*. The adjective *residential* refers to places where people live.

> *Most people in Shanghai **reside** in apartment buildings.*

> *All of the **residents** of my village work nearby.*

> *We'll be moving to a new **residence** next month.*

> ***Residential** property is expensive in big cities.*

H. Rewrite this memo to include forms of the words *priority*, *intense*, and *reside*. Try to use other target words from this unit also. Be prepared to present your work in class.

To: The Village Rescue Team

From: Relief camp director

Re: People living in villages affected by yesterday's earthquake

The strong earthquake yesterday morning injured many people who live in nearby villages. The earthquake also destroyed many homes.

The first thing we have to do is take care of the injured people. Next, we need to set up tents where people can live until their homes are rebuilt. There is plenty to eat here, so finding more food is not so important right now.

I have asked the village leader to decide which village services should be restored and in what order. His list will help us plan our schedule.

As more people come to the relief camp, our work will probably get more difficult. Help each other and try to make the best of this very difficult time.

To: The Village Rescue Team

From: Relief camp director

Re: People living in villages affected by yesterday's earthquake

_____

_____

_____

_____

_____

_____

_____

_____

_____

Before You Read

Discuss the answers to these questions in a small group.

1. What medicines do you take when you are sick? How well do they work?

2. Did your parents or grandparents have some old-fashioned ways to treat illnesses? Did those treatments work?

3. What advertisements have you seen for medicines on TV or in magazines? What kind of promises do they make?

🔊 Read

This article from a popular science magazine describes some of the sources for new medicines.

Searching for New Medicines

Over time, new diseases develop that cannot be cured with the medicines we have. Also, many medicines that once cured common diseases sometimes lose their power to cure. For these reasons,
5 modern drug companies are constantly looking for new medicines to help doctors cure both new and common diseases. One place that drug companies are looking is in the rainforests of the world. Scientists believe that new plants from the rainforests or simple
10 medicines from rainforest peoples might be sources for future miracle drugs.

Illustration of the cinchona tree and its flowers, fruit, and bark

FINDING A CURE FOR MALARIA

Four hundred years ago, just such a miracle drug was found to cure malaria. In 1633, a fortunate event **occurred**. A man from Spain went to Peru to teach the
15 native people. While he was teaching, he learned something. The village healer—the only **medical practitioner** the people had ever known—was making a powder from the bark[1] of the cinchona tree. The healer used this powder to cure malaria. The man
20 brought some of this miracle powder home to Europe, where malaria was a serious disease at the time. Europeans began using the bark to cure malaria. Soon Europeans **implemented** overseas searches for sources of the tree bark. After many years, scientists identified the ingredient in the tree bark that
25 cured malaria. It was quinine. By 1827, quinine was commercially produced and became the primary **medical** treatment for malaria throughout the world. By the 1960s, however, quinine's ability to kill the malaria parasite had **declined** because the parasite was becoming resistant to it.

A NEW MEDICINE TO CURE MALARIA

About this time, another fortunate event **occurred**. Scientists in China were
30 digging up ancient cities. One city was a place where people had **resided** 2,000 years earlier. The scientists discovered that the ancient people had used a plant, called wormwood, to cure fevers. Scientists collected living samples of the plant to test. They found that wormwood contained

---

[1] *bark:* the hard outer covering of a tree

artemisinin. This chemical killed malaria parasites. Today,
35 artemisinin is used in various mixtures with other drugs to
treat people who have malaria.

THE HISTORY OF ASPIRIN

Aspirin is another ancient medicine. Its history dates back
over 2,000 years, when ancient Greek physicians made a
tea from willow bark to ease pain and lower fever. People
40 continued to use willow bark as a home remedy for
centuries. Modern scientists identified *salicylic acid* as the
special ingredient in the bark that eased pain and fever.
Soon, drug companies were making aspirin tablets
containing salicylic acid. Today, aspirin is one of the most
45 widely used drugs in the world. Around 100 billion aspirin
tablets are produced each year.

A vase with an image of an
ancient Greek physician.

A MODERN MIRACLE DRUG

Not all **medical** histories are centuries old. The story of
taxol is an example of how miracle drugs are still being found in the world's
forests. In 1966, scientists discovered a powerful chemical in the bark of the
50 Pacific yew tree. This chemical could stop cell growth. They believed it would
be useful in treating the unnatural cell growth of cancer. Several years later,
taxol was being used in **intensive** treatments for certain kinds of cancer.

SEARCHING THE RAINFORESTS

Scientists think that many medicines may still be hidden in the rainforests of
the world. As a result, over 100 companies that manufacture drugs are
55 searching for new rainforest plants and testing them for possible **medical** use.
Unfortunately, **access** to these rainforest plants is rapidly disappearing.
Logging companies are cutting down the rainforest trees and selling the
wood. Commercial developers are **laboring** hard to clear the land for houses,
farms, towns, and roads. Clearly, the **priorities** of the scientists **conflict** with
60 the **priorities** of the loggers and the developers. The scientists want time to
find plants that might cure diseases. The loggers and developers want to
make money. They do not want to wait for the scientists to look for plants.

WILL CURES BE LOST?

Experts believe that about 50,000 types of plants, animals, and insects
disappear every year because rainforests are being destroyed. Scientists
65 fear that when rainforest species disappear, many possible cures for
diseases will disappear with them. They also fear that when rainforests
disappear, the villages of native people who **reside** in the rainforests will
also disappear. When the people leave, their healers also leave. These
practitioners are the only individuals who know the secrets of healing sick
70 people with forest plants.

THE SEARCH IS ON

In fact, most modern drugs made from plants came from simple cures that
village healers created from nearby plants. Also, some scientists say that over
70 percent of promising anti-cancer drugs originally came from rainforest

plants. As a result, modern drug companies are sending scientists,
75 **accompanied** by local translators, to work **cooperatively** with village
healers. The scientists want to learn their secrets before those secrets are lost
forever. Drug companies are also sending teams of workers into the
rainforests to gather plants to test. If company scientists find a useful cure in
a plant they test, they will identify the chemicals in the plant. Then, the
80 company can manufacture a medicine that is chemically identical.

Before rainforests disappear completely, scientists want to gather as many
medical secrets as possible. Soon, however, it may be too late to learn the
rainforest's secrets. ■

WORLD RAINFOREST LOCATIONS

■ Rainforest

Reading Comprehension

Mark each sentence as *T* (true) or *F* (false) according to the information in Reading 2.
Use your dictionary to check the meaning of new words.

___ 1. In 1633, Indians residing in Peru treated malaria with a powder made from
tree bark.

___ 2. Europeans had access to quinine over 2,000 years ago.

___ 3. The discovery of artemisinin occurred in the 1960s.

___ 4. Taxol is now used in the intensive treatment of malaria.

___ 5. Drug companies are implementing searches in the rainforests for new
medicinal plants.

___ 6. Logging companies are cooperating with scientists by cutting down trees.

___ 7. The priorities of rainforest loggers conflict with the priorities of scientists.

___ 8. Translators accompany scientists into the rainforests to help scientists learn
secrets from village healers.

___ 9. As rainforests disappear, the number of people living there will decline.

LEARN

Sometimes the title of an article can help you determine its main idea. Be sure to pay attention to the words in the title.

The main idea of an article, or of a paragraph within an article, is not always stated clearly in one sentence. Sometimes you have to add or remove words.

APPLY

Answer these questions about the main idea of Reading 2 and the main ideas of the paragraphs.

1. Does the title *Searching for New Medicines* help you find the main idea of the article in the first paragraph? What is the main idea? Write it here in your own words.

   _____

2. The main idea of paragraph 2 is its first sentence. Take out the unnecessary words and write the main idea here.

   _____

3. Complete the main idea of paragraph 3:
   The ancient people of _____ *had used* _____.

4. Complete the main idea of paragraph 4:
   Aspirin was first used _____.

5. Complete the main idea of paragraph 5:
   Taxol is an example of _____.

6. Complete the main idea of paragraph 7:
   Access to _____.

7. Write the main idea of paragraph 8 in your own words.

   _____

   _____

   _____

Vocabulary Activities   STEP I: Word Level

One person *accompanies* another person when they go somewhere together.

> My brother will **accompany** me to Indonesia.

> I will be **accompanied** by my brother.

One thing *accompanies* another thing if they are used or appear together.

> A fever often **accompanies** a cold.

The noun form, *accompaniment*, is mostly used in music.

> The guitarist played with a piano **accompaniment**.

CORPUS

A. With a partner, match each item in the first column with the thing that it usually accompanies. Take turns making sentences with the information.

_a_ 1. washing instructions   a. a new shirt

     *Washing instructions usually **accompany** a new shirt.*

___ 2. dosage instructions   b. a frozen pizza

___ 3. operating instructions   c. a computer program

___ 4. cooking instructions   d. a bottle of aspirin

___ 5. watering instructions   e. an electronic appliance

___ 6. installation instructions   f. a flowering plant

B. Use the target vocabulary from the box to complete this story. Use the words in parentheses to help you.

access to	declined	occurred	priority
accompanied	labored	practitioners	resided

Ignaz Semmelweis received his medical degree in Vienna in 1844. He took a job as head of a hospital department where women went to give birth to their babies. After giving birth, the new mothers _____ in one of two large rooms

(1. *lived*)

while they recovered. In one of the rooms, many new mothers died of childbed fever, an infection inside their bodies that often _____ childbirth

(2. *went along with*)

many years ago.

In the second room, few women died. Semmelweis tried to understand why more deaths _____ in the first room. Some people blamed bad air,

(3. *happened*)

but Semmelweis noticed that the first room was very dirty. The second room was very clean. He reasoned that something in the dirt was causing the infection. Semmelweis _____ for weeks to improve the first room. Cleanliness

(4. *worked hard*)

became a _____ .

(5. *matter of great importance*)

Doctors wearing bloody clothes could not have _____ the

(6. *contact with*)

patients. Nurse _____ and doctors had to wash their hands with a

(7. *workers*)

strong chemical before examining patients. Soon, the death rate

_____ in the first room.

(8. *went down*)

The word *decline* usually refers to something becoming weaker, slower, or not as good.

    *Grandfather's health is **declining**. (verb)*

    *His doctor noticed a **decline** in his weight. (noun)*

The verb *decline* is also used to reject or refuse something. For example, you might *decline an invitation*, or *decline to answer questions*.

CORPUS

C. With a partner, decide which of these things might decline as a person grows older. Take turns making sentences with the items you selected.

*A person's eyesight might **decline**.*

✓ eyesight   ___ income   ___ amount of sleep needed

___ doctor visits   ___ TV viewing   ___ time spent with family

___ intelligence   ___ appetite   ___ sense of humor

___ energy level   ___ interests   ___ patience

As a verb, *access* means "to get or use something."

> *Doctors use the Internet to **access** information about new medicines.*
>
> *I couldn't **access** my email.*

As a noun, the word often occurs in the phrase *have access to* something, which means "to be able to get or use something."

> *Patients need to **have access to** information about the drugs they are taking.*

The adjective form is often used in relation to people who lack certain abilities.

> *These bathrooms are **accessible** to students in wheelchairs.*

or

> *These bathrooms are wheelchair **accessible**.*

The negative form is *inaccessible*.

CORPUS

D. With a partner, match the item on the left with what it can help you access. Take turns making sentences with the information.

a 1. ladder   a. a high shelf

*You need a ladder to **access** a high shelf.*

___ 2. password   b. the school library

___ 3. key   c. the subway train

___ 4. elevator   d. the top floor of the building

___ 5. ticket   e. your email

___ 6. student ID card   f. a locked closet

To *occur* means to happen or to take place. The noun form is *occurrence*.

CORPUS

E. With a partner, decide when these events *occur*. Match the event on the left with when it occurs. Take turns making sentences with the information.

a 1. hot weather   a. in the summer

*Hot weather **occurs** in the summer.*

___ 2. a full moon   b. in the morning

___ 3. midnight   c. in the middle of the week

___ 4. breakfast   d. every 28 days

___ 5. Wednesday   e. during a rainstorm

___ 6. thunder   f. at 12:00 at night

To *cooperate* with someone means that you will work together to do a job. The noun form is *cooperation*. The adjective is *cooperative* and the adverb is *cooperatively*.

> Doctors **cooperated** with scientists to develop a new drug.
> They worked **cooperatively**. It was a **cooperative** effort.
> Their **cooperation** resulted in an effective new medicine.

CORPUS

F. Imagine that you are the Minister of Health in a country where malaria is a serious problem. In your notebook, write a letter to Dr. Long, who is the Minister of Health in a neighboring country. Suggest three ways that your two countries could cooperate to save people's lives.

The verb *implement* means "to start using a plan, system, etc." The noun *implement* means "tool."

CORPUS

G. In your notebook, list examples of implements for writing, eating, cutting, and cleaning. List as many examples as you can. Discuss your ideas with a partner.

H. Self-Assessment Review: Go back to page 17 and reassess your knowledge of the target vocabulary. How has your understanding of the words changed? What words do you feel most comfortable with now?

Writing and Discussion Topics

With a partner or small group, share ideas about the following topics. Then have each person write a paragraph about one of the topics.

1. Reading 1 describes the cycle of malaria: from mosquito to person and back to mosquito. Describe another cycle of malaria: how malaria intensifies poverty and how poverty intensifies malaria.

2. What are some things that people can do to keep themselves healthy? What are some things that people can do to feel better if they get sick?

3

They Know What You Want

In this unit, you will

> read about strategies people use to market products.
> read about how products are named.
> review finding the main idea.
> increase your understanding of the target academic words for this unit.

READING SKILL Scanning

Self-Assessment

Think about how well you know each target word, and check (✓) the appropriate column. I have…

TARGET WORDS	never seen the word before	seen the word but am not sure what it means	seen the word and understand what it means	used the word, but am not sure if correctly	used the word confidently in *either* speaking *or* writing	used the word confidently in *both* speaking *and* writing
AWL						
administrate						
🔑 channel						
🔑 convince						
🔑 domestic						
explicit						
🔑 export						
implicit						
🔑 income						
innovate						
invoke						
🔑 publish						
🔑 sector						
🔑 sex						
🔑 survey						

🔑 Oxford 3000™ keywords

Before You Read

Read these questions. Discuss your answers in a small group.

1. Where do you see advertisements? Think of as many types of places as you can. Where do you see the most ads?

2. Has an advertisement ever persuaded you to buy a product? Describe the ad and the product.

3. If you invented a new product, what do you think would be the best way to introduce it to buyers?

◀)) Read

This introduction to a marketing textbook discusses the different ways that marketing reaches customers.

They Know What You Want

With her shopping list in hand, a supermarket customer is facing the challenge of selecting a breakfast cereal for her family. The shelves are stocked with as many as 200 varieties. Should she buy wheat, corn, rice, bran, or oat cereal? Sweetened or plain? With added

5 vitamins? With a plastic toy in the box for her kids? Or should she buy the one she has a discount coupon for, or the one with the funny ad on TV, or the one that is on sale?

INFLUENCING SHOPPERS' CHOICES

The shopper's ultimate choice is likely to be determined by some factor other than taste.

10 Marketers create clever ways to persuade shoppers to buy one product instead of another. Often these have little to do with the food inside the boxes. Instead, they are only to attract shoppers.

DEFINING MARKETING

15 Marketing is a company's plan for selling a product. A marketing plan, **administered** by a marketing director, includes what to name the product, how to advertise it, how to price it, how to package it, and how to **convince** customers to buy it. In short, the goal of marketing is to **channel**

20 a shopper's choices toward a single, specific product.

A marketing plan often begins with a **survey** to determine who is most likely to buy a certain type of product. Factors such as the **sex**, age, education, and **income** of
25 future customers are considered. Then, a marketing team designs a plan aimed at a specific **sector** of the population, the group that they think is most likely to buy the product.

SELLING A NEW PRODUCT

30 Selling a cereal, a garden tool, a ballpoint pen, and a designer wristwatch will obviously call for different marketing techniques. Good health may sell cereals but not pens; while humor may sell pens, but not watches. Reliable performance sells garden tools and pens, but not cereals. Rich people buy expensive watches. Students buy
35 pens. Marketing teams must consider such factors when they design a marketing campaign.

Suppose that a company has developed an **innovative** new product: a powder made from dried fruit. When mixed with warm water, the powder becomes a creamy fruit sauce for babies. Although babies will be the ones to
40 eat the product, it is their parents who will buy it. The company's marketing plan will be aimed at the parents, specifically the mothers.

SELECTING A SLOGAN

A **survey** indicates that most mothers have two top priorities: 1. They want their babies to be healthy; 2. They want to be good mothers. Marketers use this information to create a name for the new baby food: Healthy Start.
45 They also create a marketing slogan: *Give your baby a Healthy Start*. This slogan has both an **explicit** and an **implicit** message. It **explicitly** directs a mother to feed a Healthy Start meal to her baby. It also implies that this will make her a good mother because she will be giving her baby a healthy start in life.

ADVERTISING THE NEW PRODUCT

50 The marketing team then decides how and where to sell Healthy Start baby fruit. They must decide where to **publish** advertisements and what the ads should say. Maybe the ads will **invoke** the authority of a
55 famous baby doctor to emphasize the health appeal. The ads will certainly emphasize things like good taste, easy preparation, and high nutrition. Maybe the ads will include coupons for free samples.

OTHER CONSIDERATIONS

60 Maybe the marketing team will try something **innovative,** like offering a Healthy Start college scholarship to a lucky winner. The team must also decide if the focus will be on **domestic** sales or if the baby food will be

exported to foreign countries. A design company is already designing an attractive package for the product. The marketing team will test the name,
65 slogan, ads, and packaging by showing them to mothers and **surveying** their responses.

Finally, the new product will be placed on supermarket shelves. If the marketing was effective, mothers will select Healthy Start from the dozens of baby foods on the shelves. ■

Reading Comprehension

Mark each sentence as *T* (True) or *F* (False) according to the information in Reading 1. Use your dictionary to check the meaning of new words.

___ 1. A marketing director administers a marketing plan.

___ 2. A marketing plan includes ways to convince shoppers to buy a product.

___ 3. Sex, age, income, and education are some of the factors that divide the population into different sectors.

___ 4. A survey of mothers indicates that they want to be happy and want their babies to be smart.

___ 5. A marketing slogan can have both an explicit and an implicit message.

___ 6. Ads published in magazines might invoke the authority of a famous woman who is also a mother.

___ 7. Marketing teams only think about domestic sales of their products and not about exporting them.

___ 8. Offering a scholarship would be an innovative way to sell a new product.

READING SKILL   Scanning

LEARN

Students often need to find specific information from a text that they have already read. Instead of rereading the entire text, you can *scan* the article to find the information you need. *Scanning* means quickly passing your eyes over a text to notice specific things.

Think about what to scan for in order to find specific information.

To find . . .	scan the text for . . .
names	capital letters
dates	numbers and capital letters
statistics	numbers and symbols
lists	a set of words separated by commas
specific words	capital letters, letter combinations, words in *italic* or **bold**

APPLY

Scan Reading 1 for the answers to these questions. Before you scan, decide what you should scan for in each case.

1. How many types of cereal does the supermarket sell? _____
2. What factors are considered in a survey? _____
3. What is one top priority for mothers? _____
4. What is the other top priority for mothers? _____
5. What is the name of the product? _____
6. What is the slogan for the product? _____
7. Will the marketing team export the product? _____

Vocabulary Activities   STEP I: Word Level

A. With a partner, use the target words to complete these analogies. Then write the type of relationship each analogy has: example, synonym, antonym, action, or part (see Unit 1 for more on analogies).

administer	implicit	sex
export	income	publish

                                                                Relationship

1. red : color AS female : _____   _____
2. radio program : broadcast AS newspaper : _____   _____
3. take in : import AS send out : _____   _____
4. direct : indirect AS explicit : _____   _____
5. find : discover AS manage : _____   _____
6. spend : money AS earn : _____   _____

B. With a partner, use the target vocabulary in the box to complete the report. Use the words in parentheses to help you.

administrators	explicit	published	surveys
domestic	implicit	sector	

_____ show that the _____ of society that washes
   (1. studies)   (2. part)

the most dishes consists of women with children. Accordingly, marketing

_____ target that sector when they design advertisements for a
   (3. managers)

dishwashing liquid. The ads are _____ alongside other ads for
                                          (4. printed for the public)

_____ products in magazines that primarily women read. Ads like
    (5. home)

these often show a happy, smiling woman washing dishes.

Many women feel that such ads are unfair. They acknowledge that the

_____ meaning is true: the soap *does* clean your dishes. They
  (6. clear and direct)

believe, however, that the _____ message is that washing dishes is
                (7. hidden and indirect)

fun instead of work.

To *channel* something means "to make something move along a particular
path or route." A *channel* is the path or route. It is often used to describe
water or communications pathways. A television station is also called a
channel.

> She **channels** her creative energy into her art.
>
> This area has flood **channels** that carry rainwater to the ocean.
>
> If we can't settle this conflict, we will go through legal **channels** to find an
> answer.
>
> **Channel** 5 has the best local news programming.

CORPUS

C. With a partner, choose one item from each column to create logical examples of
a *channel*. Then take turns making sentences with the information.

Signs channel hotel guests to their rooms.

~~signs~~	donations	to a customer's table
airlines	food and drinks	to needy families
waiters	passengers	~~to their rooms~~
arteries	~~hotel guests~~	through the body
charities	blood	through security checks

D. With a partner, imagine that you work for a marketing agency. You have a list of
questions to ask people about their habits. Match each question to the people
you would survey. Take turns making sentences with the information.

_a_ 1. What do you spend on groceries each week? a. shoppers in a grocery store

*We could **survey** shoppers in a grocery store.*

___ 2. What are your plans after graduating?   b. people entering a theater

___ 3. What kinds of books do you like to read? c. passengers in an airport

___ 4. How often do you travel by airplane?   d. students at a university

___ 5. What kind of movies do you like?   e. readers in a library

Vocabulary Activities | STEP II: Sentence Level

Word Form Chart			
Noun	**Verb**	**Adjective**	**Adverb**
innovation innovator	innovate	innovative	innovatively

An *innovation* is the creation of something new, such as a machine, method, style or idea. To *innovate* is to introduce something new. A person who creates the *innovation* is an *innovator*. The adjective *innovative* can describe the person or the creation.

*The computer was an amazing **innovation**. It led to other **innovative** products.*

CORPUS

E. Complete this story using different forms of *innovate*.

Marketers know that (1) _____ advertising is one way

to get the attention of buyers. This means that effective marketers try to

(2) _____ when they create a marketing plan. One

(3) _____ created a process to print ads on the shells of

eggs. Egg farmers did not want to pay for this (4) _____ .

Grocery stores didn't either. Finally, a TV station agreed to pay to have

their programs advertised on eggs.

It's too soon to know if this (5) _____ will successfully

sell other products. One shopper complained, "Don't (6) _____

with my eggs! I have to eat them!"

When a person or evidence persuades you, then you are *convinced*. The arguments or evidence was *convincing*.

> I read a **convincing** article about climate change. I'm **convinced** it's real.
>
> The witnesses at the trial were **unconvincing**. I'm still **unconvinced** that they saw what happened.

F. Restate these sentences in your notebook, using the form of *convince* in parentheses. Compare sentences with a partner.

1. Health professionals believe that obesity is a serious problem. (*are convinced*)

   *Health professionals **are convinced** that obesity is a serious problem.*

2. They want people to change the way they eat. (*convince*)

3. They have good evidence that junk foods are to blame. (*convincing*)

4. Food companies advertise in a believable way that junk foods will make us happy. (*convincingly*)

5. Children are especially easy to persuade. (*convince*)

6. Even if an ad shows something impossible to believe, children think it is real information. (*unconvincing*)

7. Food companies do not believe that they are to blame for children's obesity. (*unconvinced*)

8. They believe it is the parents' responsibility to control their children's diet. (*unconvinced*)

To *export* something means to send it to another country and sell it there. An *export* is the product that is sold. An *exporter* is a person in the business of exporting things.

> Brazil **exports** coffee around the world.
>
> Tea is one of China's most important **exports**.
>
> **Exporters** look for inexpensive ways to transport their goods.

Exported and *exporting* can be used as adjectives.

> Many of Mexico's **exported** goods go to the United States.
>
> People in the **exporting** business need to speak several languages.

G. The chart lists a few countries in the world that export wheat. On a separate piece of paper, answer the questions about the chart in full sentences. Use the given form of *export*.

FIVE WHEAT EXPORTING COUNTRIES (2010)

Exporting Country	Amount of Wheat (In millions of tons)	Importing Countries
Canada	🌾🌾🌾🌾🌾🌾🌾🌾🌾🌾🌾🌾🌾🌾 17.5	China, Japan, Iran, South Korea
Argentina	🌾🌾🌾🌾🌾🌾 8.5	Brazil, Indonesia
Ukraine	🌾🌾🌾🌾 5.5	Middle East, North Africa
Kazakhstan	🌾🌾🌾🌾 5.0	South East Asia, China
Russia	🌾🌾🌾🌾 4.0	Egypt, Syria, Iran, Libya

1. Which countries imported wheat from Argentina? (*exported*)

   *Argentina **exported** wheat to Brazil and Indonesia.*

2. Which of these countries sent the most wheat? (*largest exporter*)

3. Which country sent wheat to Egypt? (*exported*)

4. Which countries were selling wheat to China? (*exporting*)

5. How much wheat did Ukraine send overseas in 2010? (*exported*)

6. What is one thing that Canada sends overseas to Japan? (*exports,* noun)

To *publish* something means to make it available to the public. Copies of books, magazines, newspapers, music, and computer software are some things that are published. A *publisher* is a person or company that produces the work.

> *The* Los Angeles Times *newspaper is **published** every day.*

 CORPUS

H. Look at the title page of this book and on the back of that same page. What is the name of the publisher of this book? In what year was the book published?

_____

_____

Before You Read

Read these questions. Discuss your answers in a small group.

1. Many automobiles are named for animals, such as Cougar or Jaguar. Would you buy an automobile named Turtle? How about Elephant? Why or why not?

2. What factors would you consider if you were responsible for naming a new product?

3. Does the name of a new product help you decide whether to try it? Why or why not?

🔊 **Read**

This excerpt from a marketing textbook discusses the factors that go into choosing a good name for a new product.

What's in a Name?

One of the most important tasks in marketing a new product is giving it a name. In marketing, the quality of a product is not as important as the quality of the name it is given. This is because marketing is not about the
5   product; it is about *selling* the product. Marketers use strategies such as attractive packaging, catchy slogans, and other clever ways to **convince** consumers to buy their product. The most powerful marketing strategy, however, is giving a product a powerful name.

RULE 1

10 To be powerful, the name must be easy to remember. In the early days of computers, there were several competing brands on the market, including Apple II, Commodore Pet, IMSAI 8080, MITS Altair 8800, and Radio Shack TRS-80. In those days, most buyers knew very little about computers, so they were not able to judge the quality of one over the
15 other. As a result, they rejected the computers with complex names. Instead, they chose the brands that **invoked** something familiar. They chose, of course, the Apple II.

RULE 2

The name must also be easy to pronounce. If customers can't pronounce the name of a product, they won't buy it. A short name is easier to
20 remember and to pronounce. According to research done by Strategic Name Development consultants, the best names have three or fewer syllables, such as Tums (antacid tablets), Xerox (copiers), or Cheerios (cereal). Many well-known names are longer, of course, such as Mercedes-Benz (automobiles) and Coca-Cola (soft drinks), so length is not the only factor.

RULE 3

25 A product name should be unique. It shouldn't sound like the name of any other product, especially a competing product. Shoppers tend to confuse Breyer's Ice Cream with Dreyer's Ice Cream and Rolex (watches) with Rolodex (desk indexes), for example.

RULE 4

In addition, an effective name should hint at what the product is used for.
For example, Sleepeez is a sleeping medication and Windex is a window
cleaner. A name should also be appropriate for the type of product it
represents. Names of medicines should sound medical, names of foods
should sound tasty, and names of **domestic** cleaning products should
sound hard-working.

RULE 5

An effective name also includes words, or parts
of words, that are positive and inviting.
Sometimes, the product name sounds like
another descriptive word that has a positive
meaning. The pain reliever Aleve, for example,
sounds like "relieve." Band-Aid (a small plastic
bandage) sounds a bit like "bandage" and
includes the word "aid." Frequently, names of
products aimed at high-**income** consumers
implicitly advertise luxury. Consider the names
of these cruise ship companies: Crystal,
Princess, Royal Caribbean, and Celebrity.

RULE 6

The letters within names are important, too. A **survey administrated** by
the above consultants asked English speakers about their reactions to
various letters of the alphabet. The results showed that people associate
the letters C, S, and B with something traditional, but associate the letters
Q, V, X, and Z with something **innovative**. Additionally, people in the
survey associated certain letters with one **sex** or the other. They considered
the letters F, L, V, and W feminine, but the letters M, X, and Z masculine.
It is not clear how those **surveyed** might react to the automobile names
Volvo, Mazda, or Lexus.

A product name should . . .

1. be easy to remember
2. be easy to pronounce
3. be unique
4. hint at what the product is for
5. include positive words or word parts
6. contain effect letters
7. translate well into other languages
8. have no negative associations

RULE 7

Marketers must also consider how a product name will translate in other
languages if the product is **exported**. A famous example of this occurred
when the Chevrolet Nova automobile was **exported** to Argentina in the
1970s. Some people predicted that it would sell poorly because in Spanish
the two words "No va" mean "It doesn't go." Fortunately, "nova" (a bright

star) is the same word in both Spanish and English and the car sold well.

RULE 8

Finally, a name must not generate negative associations in the minds of consumers. Many
65 words have an **implicit** message as well as an **explicit** meaning. Why, for example, has no car manufacturer named a car the Elephant? Elephants are big, strong, and dependable, but they are also slow-moving, huge, and eat a lot.
70 There used to be a weight-loss product called Ayds. It disappeared once AIDS became a serious illness worldwide.

Corporations put forth great effort to find the right name for a new product. They often hire consultants who specialize in creating product names. Working with the principles above, they create several
75 possible names. Then, they **channel** the names through one or more focus groups. These groups are made up of individuals drawn from the **sector** of the population that is most likely to buy the target product, such as, sports fans, frequent travelers, or senior citizens. When a focus group meets, they freely discuss what they like or don't like about the
80 possible names.

Once the right name is chosen, advertisements are widely **published** to introduce the new product to the buying public. Only time will tell if the important marketing decisions made earlier will be effective in selling the product. ▪

Reading Comprehension

Mark each sentence as *T* (True) or *F* (False) according to Reading 2. Use your dictionary to focus on the meaning of new words.

____ 1. A powerful name helps convince consumers to buy a product.

____ 2. Early computer buyers chose a brand name that invoked high-tech innovation.

____ 3. The names of domestic cleaning products should sound hard-working.

____ 4. Many words have an implicit message as well as an explicit meaning.

____ 5. A survey administered by naming consultants showed that product names spelled with an X are considered innovative.

____ 6. A product name must be changed if the product is exported to other countries.

____ 7. High-income car buyers would be likely to buy a luxury car named Elephant.

____ 8. Naming consultants channel possible product names through focus groups drawn from the sector of the population most likely to buy the target product.

APPLY

A. Scanning is useful for finding examples. Scan Reading 2 to find this information.

1. the number of product names that include an X: _____

2. the number of product names that include a V: _____

3. the number of product names that include a Z: _____

B. Scan the article again to find out what kind of product each of these is or was.

1. Celebrity _____
2. Pet _____
3. Aleve _____
4. Rolodex _____
5. Ayds _____
6. Windex _____
7. Cheerios _____
8. Nova _____
9. Tums _____
10. Breyer's _____

REVIEW A SKILL   **Finding the Main Idea** (See pp. 21, 29)

In the first paragraph of Reading 2, find the sentence that states the main idea of the article. Look at the first sentence of the following paragraphs. How is each one related to the main idea of the article?

Vocabulary Activities   STEP I: Word Level

To *invoke* can mean simply to ask for help or support from someone. More commonly, it is used when someone wants to mention or quote an authority to support an action or opinion.

> The author **invoked** the works of leading scholars to support his arguments.

Advertisements often invoke the authority of powerful people or institutions to convince customers to buy their product.

> The ads for the new dictionary **invoke** the authority of professors from several universities.

CORPUS

A. With a partner, decide what product each advertisement might be for. What sector of buyers is the ad probably targeting? What authority does each ad invoke? Then think of another type of product and write an ad for it together. Be sure to invoke a convincing authority.

1. "When the Olympic hockey team needs a burst of energy, they grab a *Champ* and keep on going!"

Product: _____

Sector: _____

2. "Celebrity chef Michelangelo Sotto uses only the best ingredients in his spaghetti sauce. That's why he uses new *Multo, Multo*."

   Product: _____

   Sector: _____

3. "Scholars and academics across the country turn to *WordPower*—because accuracy matters."

   Product: _____

   Sector: _____

4. "The Association of Children's Dentists recommends *Glisten* over all other competitors."

   Product: _____

   Sector: _____

5. "Professional race car drivers depend on *Nexosol*—the fuel of champions!"

   Product: _____

   Sector: _____

6. Product: _____

   Sector: _____

   Ad: _____

B. Imagine that you are completing a survey to be part of a focus group. The marketing consultants want to find out about you so they can channel you to the right group. Create an imaginary person and complete this application with imaginary information. Mark your answers with an X.

Age	Sex	Income	Education	Home
☐ Under 20	☐ Male	☐ Under $30,000	☐ Elementary School	☐ Owner
☐ 20–25	☐ Female	☐ $30,000–$50,000	☐ Secondary School	☐ Renter
☐ 25–40		☐ $50,000–$75,000	☐ University	
☐ 40–60		☐ over $75,000		
☐ over 60				

A message that is *explicit* is one that is clearly and directly stated. An *implicit* message is one that is not directly stated.

Explicit message: *Go home.*

Implicit message: *It's getting late. Let's talk more tomorrow.*

CORPUS

C. Imagine that you are meeting with clients who are important to your advertising business. Everyone wants to be polite. With a partner, match the *implicit* statement on the left with the *explicit* message that has the same meaning.

___ 1. Excuse me for yawning.
___ 2. It's a little cold in here.
___ 3. Let me review the costs.
___ 4. Shall we break for lunch?
___ 5. I want to think about that.
___ 6. Is this date correct?

a. Don't open that window.
b. You made a mistake.
c. I don't know the answer.
d. That's too much money.
e. I'm bored. / I'm tired.
f. I'm hungry.

Vocabulary Activities STEP II: Sentence Level

Domestic refers to the home and family or to a home country. It can be used in many different contexts. The adjective is *domesticated*.

> Those items are necessary to satisfy his family's basic **domestic** needs.
> **Domestic** postal rates are lower than overseas rates.
> My country exports 25% of **domestically** grown fruits and vegetables.
> Scientists say that **domesticated** animals live longer than wild animals.

CORPUS

D. Rewrite these sentences in your notebook using a form of *domestic*. Compare sentences with a partner.

1. Few families can afford to hire someone to help with household chores.

   *Not all families can afford to hire someone to help with **domestic** chores.*

2. Farmers often have many tame animals, such as sheep and goats.

3. Every summer our store has a sale on products for the home.

4. You should arrive at the airport two hours before flights within the country.

5. Coffee must be imported from other countries because it is not grown here.

To *administer* means to control and manage the giving of something. For example, a doctor administers medicine to patients, or a teacher administers a test to students.

The most common usage of this word family, however, is for business and politics:

administrator	a manager in a company, organization, or government
administration	the work done by administrators
the administration	the group of people managing an organization or government

> The school **administrator** was pleased with the success of the innovative programs she has implemented across the city.
> The director oversaw the **administration** of the new safety rules.
> The **administration** has been criticized for wasting taxpayers' money.

Administrative refers to the work of administering services, or office work in general. *Administratively* is the adverb.

> The chief of police has an **administrative** role in the police department.
> My brother is the **administrative** assistant for the whole department.
> The fire department is **administratively** separate from the city government.

CORPUS

E. Read the chart showing some of the employees of Black's Button Company. Then answer the questions that follow in your notebook. Include the form of *administer* indicated in each sentence.

Name	Title	Area of Responsibility
Jerry Green	Plant Manager	safety and maintenance of the factory
Marie Brown	Administrative Assistant	secretary to Fred Black
Fred Black	Chief Executive Officer	operation of the entire company
Ellen White	Marketing Director	marketing
Jane Gray	Human Resources Director	employment office

1. What does Marie Brown do? (*administratively*)

   She assists Mr. Black **administratively**.

2. Who is Fred Black? (*administrator*)

3. What does Ellen White do? (*administrative responsibility*)

4. What does Jane Gray do? (*administers*)

5. What does Jerry Green do? (*administration*)

F. Which of the jobs in the chart in activity E would you be best at? Why? What are your administrative strengths and weaknesses? In your noteboook, write a short paragraph in which you explain your answers. Be prepared to present your work in class.

G. Self-Assessment Review: Go back to page 33 and reassess your knowledge of the target vocabulary. How has your understanding of the words changed? What words do you feel most comfortable with now?

Writing and Discussion Topics

With a partner or small group, share ideas about the following topics. Then have each person write a paragraph about one of the topics.

1. Reading 2 mentions several rules for naming a product. Think of some successful products whose names do not follow these rules. Why do you think they are successful anyway?

2. Describe an advertisement that you like from a magazine. What sector of the public do you think is the target market? How does this ad try to convince the target market to buy the product? Is it innovative in some way? If so, how?

3. Think of the many ways that a product could be advertised, such as on TV or in a magazine, for example. What are the advantages of each way?

Identifying People

In this unit, you will

> read about the importance of titles in identifying people.
> review scanning a text.
> increase your understanding of the target academic words for this unit.

READING SKILL Identifying Examples

Self-Assessment

Think about how well you know each target word, and check (✓) the appropriate column. I have…

TARGET WORDS	never seen the word before	seen the word but am not sure what it means	seen the word and understand what it means	used the word, but am not sure if correctly	used the word confidently in *either* speaking *or* writing	used the word confidently in *both* speaking *and* writing
AWL						
🔑 acquire						
ambiguous						
analogy						
🔑 civil						
constitute						
🔑 context						
convene						
differentiate						
🔑 index						
integral						
🔑 military						
🔑 somewhat						
🔑 style						
🔑 via						
whereby						

🔑 Oxford 3000™ keywords

Before You Read

Read these questions. Discuss your answers in a small group.

1. Do you have a nickname? Who calls you by this name?

2. If you had a problem at school or at your job, who would you ask for help?

3. Name some people in your neighborhood that wear uniforms.

Read

This excerpt from a sociology textbook discusses group membership.

Who Are You?

Imagine that you read the following story in your local newspaper.

Yoshi Tanaka was injured at the Pacifica Café when the chair he was sitting on broke. Angelo Manzoli said his career is ruined. Carlos Armada claimed that Tanaka was to blame. Fred
5　Katz said his crew helped transport the 450-pound man to a hospital. Ahmed Nadel said Tanaka was not seriously hurt.

Who are these people? If we give each a title, the **ambiguous** story becomes easier to understand.

Sumo wrestler Yoshi Tanaka was injured at the Pacifica Café
10　when the chair he was sitting on broke. His trainer, Angelo Manzoli, said his career is ruined. Carlos Armada, owner of the café, claimed that Tanaka was to blame. Fire Chief Fred Katz said his crew helped transport the 450-pound man to a hospital. Physician Dr. Ahmed Nadel said Tanaka was not seriously hurt.

GROUPS

15　Throughout our lives, and even during a single day, we are part of many groups. These groups might include a family, an orchestra, a team, a business, a school, a country, or even a temporary group such as the people affected by a café accident.

TITLES

Within a group, titles help **differentiate** one person from another. Each
20　person is an **integral** part of many different groups, so each person has many titles. For instance, a man might be an engineer, a husband, a father, a son, a brother, the coach of his son's baseball team, a tennis club member, a conservative voter, and an Internet chat room visitor. The title *engineer*

defines his status within the **context** of employment. The titles *husband,*
father, son, and *brother* define his status within the **context** of family.

ADDRESSING OTHERS

Titles also provide guidelines **whereby** people know how to address others. At
work, the engineer's co-workers call him Jim, but people who phone his
company will ask to speak to Jim Wilson. His wife calls him Honey, and his
children call him Dad. His mother still calls him Jimmy, a childhood nickname,
and his brother affectionately calls him Jimbo. The baseball team kids call
him Coach Wilson. His tennis partner calls him Wilson. Mail he receives from
his political party is addressed to Mr. James Wilson. On the Internet, he's
known as J.W.

CULTURAL DIFFERENCES

Rules for how people address each other vary from one culture to another. In
Japanese culture, for example, only family and close friends call someone by
his or her given name. It is considered rude to call someone by just his family
name. A family name must be followed by the title *-san,* so Mr. or Ms. Tanaka
is known as Tanaka-san. When addressing someone of
a higher status, often no name is used. Instead this
person is addressed by his or her title, such as
teacher or *company president.*

JOB TITLES

The title *company president* clearly refers to the leader
of a company. Among its employees, a company
differentiates between the types of workers **via** job
titles like *lab technician, secretary,* or *department*
supervisor. A person's job title also serves as an **index**
(or measure) of his or her status within the company.
Employees with a higher status are usually paid a
higher salary. Similarly, if an employee earns a raise in
salary, he or she is often given a new job title.

LEADERS' TITLES

The leader of a group of people almost always has
a title. For instance, clubs have presidents, teams
have captains, committees have chairmen or
chairwomen, stores have managers, fire
departments have chiefs, and schools have
principals. Every **civil** leader has a title, too,
though these vary **somewhat** depending on a
country's system of government. These titles
include *prime minister, president, governor, sultan,*
and *king.* When official meetings **convene,** the
leaders are addressed in a formal **style,** such as
Madam President or *Governor Ramos.*

Job Posting		
TITLE	**LOCATION**	**POSTED**
President Construction	Dubai	1 day ago
Secretary Marketing	New York	2 days ago
Lab Technician Pharmaceutical	Tokyo	5 days ago
Accounts Manager Advertising	London	1 week ago
Art Director Publishing	Frankfurt	2 weeks ago
Analyst Media	Madrid	3 weeks ago

**Chancellor Angela Merkel and Prime Minister
Sheikh Hasina**

INHERITED TITLES

Some titles are **acquired** by inheritance. These include the royal male titles *king, emperor,* and *sultan* and their **analogous** female

65 titles *queen, empress,* and *sultana.* Leaders of tribes and clans may inherit titles such as *khan, sheikh,* and *chief.* A given name plus the inherited title usually **constitute** their public names, such as King Faisal or Queen Elizabeth. Often they are addressed in special ways, like *Your Highness.*

MILITARY TITLES

70 Titles are especially important in the **military**, where authority is channeled from top to bottom **via** a strict chain of command. A common ranking system in armies begins at the top with the title *field marshal* or *general,* and ends with the lowest rank of *soldier.*

Titles are important tools that help us understand the status of members

75 within human groups.

Reading Comprehension

Mark each sentence as *T* (true) or *F* (false) according to the information in Reading 1. Use your dictionary to check the meaning of new words.

____ 1. The acquired title *king* for a man is analogous to the title *queen* for a woman.

____ 2. The title *engineer* defines a person's status in the context of family.

____ 3. Titles provide guidelines whereby people know how to address others.

____ 4. Each person is an integral part of many different groups.

____ 5. Titles are somewhat important in the military.

____ 6. Companies differentiate between types of workers via job titles.

____ 7. When official meetings convene, civil leaders are addressed in a formal style.

____ 8. A given name plus an inherited title constitute the public name of Queen Elizabeth.

____ 9. The titles *field marshal* and *general* are ambiguous.

____10. A job title is an index of an employee's status in a company.

READING SKILL   Identifying Examples

LEARN

One way that writers make their ideas clear is by giving examples. Sometimes an entire text is made up of examples, with each paragraph giving a different kind of example to support the main idea of the reading. There might also be several examples within one paragraph to help explain the ideas in that paragraph.

Reading 1 uses examples in both of these ways. You can identify examples in a text by looking for certain signals. Here are some common words and phrases that signal examples:

for example	for instance	such as
including	these include	one is…
like	there are many kinds of…	another is…

APPLY

Refer to Reading 1 to answer these questions.

1. What kinds of examples are discussed in the paragraph titled "Groups"?

   _____

2. What words are used to introduce the examples in the paragraph titled "Groups"?

   _____

3. What signal words are used in the paragraph titled "Cultural Differences" to introduce the examples?

   _____

4. What signal words are used in the paragraph titled "Job Titles" to introduce the examples?

   _____

5. What signal words are used in the paragraph titled "Leaders' Titles" to introduce the examples?

   _____

REVIEW A SKILL Scanning (See p. 36)

Scan Reading 1. How many times does the word *president* occur? Scan the paragraph titled "Addressing Others". How many different names does the engineer have?

Vocabulary Activities STEP I: Word Level

A. Use the target vocabulary in the box to complete this story. Use the words in parentheses to help you.

acquired	context	integral	via
constituted	conventional	somewhat	whereby

In 1849, thousands of people went to California in search of gold, hoping to get rich. Levi Strauss, a cloth salesman, went there, too. He hoped to get rich, but in a different way. When the gold miners complained that their pants tore easily, Strauss made them pants out of strong denim cloth. The men liked the pants, but the pockets kept tearing. This _____ a problem, but a tailor had an idea
                                                (1. made)
_____ the pockets could be made stronger with copper rivets.
(2. by which)

Strauss and the tailor soon became rich—not from gold, but from inventing jeans. For the next 100 years, jeans were worn mostly by farmers or factory workers. In the 1950s, young people began wearing jeans. As a group, they made a strong statement against _____ dress _____ their jeans
(3. standard)   (4. by means of)
because jeans were considered improper by most people. In the 1960s, jeans became _____ more acceptable. In the _____ of the
(5. a little)   (6. setting)
1970s, they _____ fashion status. Today, jeans are an
(7. earned)
_____ part of the wardrobe of many young people.
(8. necessary)

Somewhat has the same meaning as "sort of" or "a little bit."

I agree **somewhat** *with what you're saying.*

His trousers were **somewhat** *wrinkled, and his shirt was torn.*

CORPUS

B. With a partner, match the person on the left with what he or she claims to be "somewhat of an expert" on. Write in your notebooks. Take turns creating sentences with the information.

1. I eat out every week   restaurants

   I eat out every week, so I'm **somewhat** *of an expert on restaurants.*

2. I've traveled overseas twice   literature

3. I used to play the piano   cars

4. My father is a mechanic   airports

5. I used to work in a bookstore   music

Via means "passing through" or "by way of a place."

I'll fly from here to Berlin **via** *Paris.*

It can also mean "by means of" or "using."

Relatives who live far from each other can keep in touch **via** *email.*

CORPUS

C. Imagine that you are the president of a large company. By what means would you communicate each of these messages to your employees? Match the messages on the left with the means on the right. Then tell a partner the reasons for your answers.

___ 1. We've had a dangerous chemical spill.   a. via a sticky note

___ 2. You haven't been doing your job. You're fired.   b. via email

___ 3. Please sign this form and return it to me.   c. via telephone

___ 4. There's a manager's meeting at 8 a.m.   d. via a face-to-face
       tomorrow.   discussion

___ 5. Please come to my office right away.

e. via the company newsletter

___ 6. Congratulations to Harry Chan on his new baby.

f. via the public address system

People in a society can be divided into two sectors: *military* and *civil*.

> Members of the army, navy, and air force constitute the **military** sector.
>
> Ordinary citizens constitute the **civil** sector.

CORPUS

D. With a partner, decide whether these are military or civil titles. Write *M* for military and *C* for civil.

___ police chief   ___ general   ___ prime minister

___ lawyer   ___ manager   ___ field marshal

___ soldier   ___ fireman   ___ lieutenant

Vocabulary Activities   STEP II: Sentence Level

To *differentiate* one thing from another means "to create a difference between them," or "to see the difference."

> Universities **differentiate** between sports for men and sports for women.
>
> It's hard to **differentiate** one brand of coffee from another.

The noun form is *differentiation*.

> **Differentiation** between military ranks is shown by stripes on uniform sleeves.

CORPUS

E. In your notebook, rewrite these sentences to include the given form of *differentiate*.

1. In most cultures, given names show a difference between males and females. (*differentiate*)

2. Often there is no change in the civil titles of males or females. (*differentiation*)

3. Civil titles help separate ordinary citizens from people in authority. (*differentiate*)

Something that is *ambiguous* is not clear in meaning, often because there is more than one possible meaning. For example, the newspaper headline "Hospital Begins Operations" is *ambiguous*. The *ambiguity* is caused by the word "operations," which has more than one meaning. "Operations" can refer to either medical surgery or services.

The headline can be rewritten to clarify the writer's meaning. Two *unambiguous* headlines are "Hospital Begins Surgery" and "Hospital Opens for Service."

F. Read these ambiguous newspaper headlines. Each has two meanings. With a partner, discuss why they are ambiguous. Then in your notebook, write two unambiguous sentences that show the two meanings.

1. President Enjoys Visiting King

   The president enjoys going to visit the king.

   The president enjoys having the king visit him.

2. Rare Monkey Eats Carrots and Flies

3. Bus Riders Miss Planes

4. Entertaining Actors Can Be Expensive

5. Biting Frogs Found Harmful

To *convene* means "to meet or come together, usually for an official or formal meeting." The noun form is *convention*.

   *The parliament **convenes** each morning at 10 a.m.*

   *I'll attend a medical **convention** in Tokyo next month.*

Convention can also mean a tradition or a standard way of behaving.

   *The Western **convention** is for a married woman to take her husband's surname.*

Something *conventional* is traditional or standard, while something *unconventional* is unusual and often disapproved of.

   *Teenagers sometime surprise adults with **unconventional** ideas.*

   *You should dress **conventionally** when you apply for a job.*

G. Write the answers to these questions in your notebook. Write in full sentences and use the word in parentheses.

1. Describe a common wedding tradition practiced in your family. (*conventionally*)

2. Describe how students at your school address their teachers. (*conventional*)

3. Describe where students at your school gather for meetings. (*convene*)

4. Describe a standard way that people greet each other. (*convention*)

Whereby means "by which" or "because of which." It is a formal way to connect two ideas. The first idea describes an action and the second part shows the result of the action.

> *Nancy went on a strict diet, **whereby** she lost 35 pounds.*

Note that *whereby* connects two full clauses.

CORPUS

H. In your notebook, complete each of these sentences with a full clause that begins with the word *whereby*. Use the story about Yoshi Tanaka at the beginning of Reading 1 as a source of ideas.

1. Yoshi Tanaka's chair broke, whereby he *fell on the floor* _____.

2. His manager saw tears in Yoshi's eyes, whereby the manager knew _____ _____.

3. The owner of the cafe claimed that Yoshi was to blame, whereby the owner avoided _____.

4. Fred Katz's crew lifted Yoshi onto a fire truck, whereby they were able _____.

5. A hospital technician took X-rays, whereby the doctor _____ _____.

The *style* of something is the way that it is done, designed, or presented.

> *I don't like the **style** of that shirt.*
>
> *Her **style** of writing is very easy to follow.*

Style usually refers to things that are created, such as a style of art, architecture, music, singing, dancing, writing, etc.

Something that is *in style* is currently popular. Something that is *out of style* is no longer popular. Fashionable clothes are said to be *stylish*.

The verb *to style* means to arrange someone's hair in an attractive way.

> *I had my hair cut and **styled** yesterday.*

CORPUS

I. On a separate piece of paper, write a sentence about someone's style of doing something that you like. Tell why you like it. Write another sentence about someone's style of doing something that you do not like. Tell why you do not like it. Choose from these topics: teaching, cooking, singing, talking, playing a sport, or choose one of your own.

Before You Read

Read these questions. Discuss your answers in a small group.

1. What jobs or social roles require people to wear special clothing?

2. What clothes do you associate with royalty (kings and queens, etc.)?

3. A flag is one symbol of a nation. What are some other things that can be used as symbols of a nation?

Read

This excerpt from a social science textbook is about the significance of clothing in a culture.

Symbolic Clothing

Hundreds of years ago, umbrellas were symbols of power and authority. Kings, sheikhs, popes, and other rulers believed that owning these sunshades added to their importance. The more umbrellas a ruler **acquired**, the more he impressed others; and, by **analogy**,
5 the bigger his umbrellas, the more power the owner appeared to have. It seems odd to us today that such an everyday object could have once been used to **differentiate** rulers from ordinary people. Yet at that time, an umbrella was an **unambiguous** symbol of power. Similarly, contemporary cultures
10 today employ many common items, including clothing, as symbols of social status.

IN UNIVERSITIES

The academic cap and gown is one example of symbolic clothing. Hundreds of years ago, university students were required to
15 wear long, black robes. Today academic robes are usually worn only for graduation ceremonies, along with a special cap. Many universities have developed their own traditional **style** and color of cap and gown.
20 For example, at some universities, students wear a close-fitting cap topped by a flat square. A tassel, which is a bundle of long silk strings, hangs from the square. By **convention**, students begin the graduation ceremony with the tassel hanging from the left side of the square. Once a university administrator declares that the students have
25 officially graduated, they move their tassels to the right side of the square to indicate their new change of status. Graduating students also wear collars or sashes of cloth over their gowns, **whereby** their field of academic specialization is indicated **via** color. These colors vary among universities

and countries. For example, in Spain a gold cloth symbolizes medicine,
while in the United States a green cloth symbolizes medicine.

IN CIVIL COURTS OF LAW

For example, in the **civil** courts of law in many countries, judges wear long
robes, usually black, that cover their ordinary clothing. The robes identify
the judges' role in the courtroom and symbolize their authority to
administer justice. The gavel that judges rap to **convene** court and maintain
order is another such symbol of authority. In Britain and in most
Commonwealth nations, judges and certain court officials also wear white
wigs that symbolize their roles.

AMONG ROYALTY

Similarly, the ceremonial clothing of kings and queens is symbolic of their
royal status. The most common symbol of royal status is a crown. The
crown is placed on the head of the new monarch during a formal
ceremony. He or she usually wears a beautiful cape made of fur, feathers,
or delicate material for the event.

WEDDING SYMBOLS

A wedding, too, is a change-of-status
ceremony. Traditional clothing is usually an
integral part of the ritual. In a **conventional**
Western wedding, the bride wears a long,
white dress. She also wears a white veil on
her head and carries a bouquet of flowers.
Her clothing and various accessories (which
may be hidden) **constitute** traditional good-
luck items that a bride should wear. These
include "something old, something new,
something borrowed, something blue, and a
lucky penny in her shoe." An important part
of the ceremony is the exchange of wedding

rings. These circles of gold or silver have no ending, and symbolize the
lifetime relationship the bride and groom are about to begin.

   The symbolism of the white wedding dress is so strong that brides from
many non-Western cultures have chosen to include such a dress in their
weddings. An Asian bride, for example, might wear a red gown during a
traditional wedding ceremony and then change into a **stylish** white wedding
dress for the celebration that follows.

UNIFORMS

A uniform identifies the occupation and status of many workers. In the
civil sector of society, for example, police officers and fire fighters wear
uniforms. So do waiters and waitresses, airline pilots and cabin stewards,
and nurses and dental assistants. With the exception of fire fighters, these
people could do their jobs just as efficiently in ordinary clothing. A
uniform, however, serves two important purposes. First, a uniform
differentiates these workers from other people. A uniform is one way
whereby the workers can be easily identified by others. Second, a uniform

is a symbol of authority, which gives people confidence in the workers. Another item of clothing that is **somewhat** of a uniform is the tall, white hat worn by chefs. This hat **conventionally** symbolizes the chef's position of authority in the **context** of a restaurant kitchen.

75   **Military** personnel, too, wear uniforms, but different types. One type is for everyday wear, and another is the formal uniform worn for **military** ceremonies. A third type is worn in battle. **Military** uniforms serve several symbolic functions. First, the various decorations on a uniform jacket and hat are **indexes** of a member's rank in the

80 **military.** Second, uniforms encourage members of a group to **acquire** a sense of unity and pride. Finally, in the **context** of a battle, uniforms become symbols of the nation the soldiers are defending.

    Symbolic clothing can symbolize many things, including authority, nationality and change of status. Often the original significance of the

85 clothing has been forgotten or has changed over time, yet societies continue to respect the **conventional** symbolism. Other clothing, such as the white wedding dress, became symbolic **somewhat** recently, yet is still considered traditional. The objects and clothing that become important symbols in a culture are determined by the special meaning that people give them. ■

Reading Comprehension

Mark each sentence as *T* (true) or *F* (false) according to the information in Reading 2. Use your dictionary to check the meaning of new words.

___ 1. Hundreds of years ago, the umbrellas that kings, sheikhs, and popes acquired became indexes of their high positions in society.

___ 2. Sometimes ambiguous symbols of power are used to differentiate between rulers and ordinary people.

___ 3. The gavel that judges rap to convene sessions in a civil court of law is a symbol of the nation they represent.

___ 4. Graduating students wear collars or sashes over their academic gowns, whereby they indicate their change of status via color.

___ 5. A long white dress and a white veil constitute the wedding clothing of a traditional Western bride.

___ 6. In some cultures, the Western wedding dress is becoming an integral part of non-Western weddings.

___ 7. In the context of a battle, uniforms become symbols of military rank.

___ 8. The symbolism of some ceremonial clothing is somewhat recent.

READING SKILL   Identifying Examples

APPLY

Refer to Reading 2 to answer these questions.

1. Reread the first paragraph of Reading 2. Find the sentence that tells you the main idea of the article, and write it here.

_____

2. Each paragraph in the article discusses a different example of symbolic clothing. Who wears the symbolic clothing mentioned in each of these paragraphs?

Paragraph 2 _____   Paragraph 5 _____

Paragraph 3 _____   Paragraph 7 _____

Paragraph 4 _____   Paragraph 8 _____

3. Paragraph 3 gives two examples of symbols of authority. What are they?

_____   _____

4. What three items constitute the traditional clothing of a bride in a Western wedding?

_____   _____   _____

5. In Paragraph 8, what words introduce three kinds of military uniforms?

_____   _____   _____

6. What words introduce the three symbolic functions of military uniforms?

_____   _____   _____

Vocabulary Activities STEP I: Word Level

Sometimes creating an *analogy* takes imagination.

*Some people see an **analogy** between the features on the outside of a house and a face. The windows are **analogous** to eyes, for example.*

CORPUS

A. How is an automobile like a person? With a partner, create analogies by matching each car part in the left column with an analogous body part on the right. Take turns saying those analogies.

_a_ 1. gasoline   a. food

   *Gasoline is **analogous** to food.*

___ 2. windshield   b. feet

___ 3. driver   c. heart

___ 4. tires   d. brain

___ 5. engine   e. stomach

___ 6. gasoline tank   f. eyes

An *index* is an indication or a measurement of something.

*The consumer price **index** shows changes in the prices of products over time.*

The *index* of a textbook helps readers locate information in the book.

*Check the **index** of your science text to see if it covers cell division.*

Note: *Indexes* is the common plural form, but sometimes *indices* is used.

CORPUS

B. Read these statements about an imaginary country. What might each statement be an *index* of? Discuss your answers in a small group.

1. Most people live to be 75 years old or more.

   *This might be an **index** of good medical care in the country.*

2. Most children of the residents go to college.

3. Almost every adult of working age has a job.

4. Ninety percent of the adults vote in elections.

C. When something is an *integral* part of a whole thing, it means that it is a necessary or required part. Complete these sentences. Refer to the information in Reading 2. Compare answers with a partner.

1. In some cultures, _____ is an integral part of the ceremonial clothing.

2. Changing the _____ is an integral part of a graduation ceremony.

3. Exchanging _____ is an integral part of a Western wedding.

4. _____ has become an integral part of some non-Western weddings.

Vocabulary Activities | STEP II: Sentence Level

Word Form Chart			
Noun	**Verb**	**Adjective**	**Adverb**
context	contextualize	context contextualized	_____

One meaning of *context* is the "circumstance or situation in which something occurs."

*A judge's robe is a symbol of authority only in the **context** of a courtroom.*

Context can also refer to the words and ideas in a text that help readers understand new or ambiguous words. Good readers use *context clues* to help them understand new or ambiguous words in a text. It is hard to learn new words in a list because the words are not *contextualized*.

In Reading 2, the context clues—academic clothing, graduation ceremony, cap—help you understand what the word "tassel" means.

CORPUS

D. Write a sentence describing the appropriate clothing to wear in each of these contexts. Use the word *context* in your sentence.

1. interviewing for a job

   *It would be appropriate to wear a suit in a business **context**.*

2. attending a wedding as a guest

3. eating dinner at an informal restaurant

4. attending a nephew or niece's high school graduation ceremony

5. going hiking in the mountains

E. Each of these words has more than one meaning. Consult your dictionary to find the different meanings. Then write a sentence in your notebook that provides a context explaining <u>one</u> meaning of each word. Compare sentences in a small group.

1. refrain

   *The guitarist sang the verses of the song and asked the audience to sing the **refrain** after each verse.*

2. game

3. orange

4. gag

5. pale

The verb *constitute* means "to make up or form something." The adjective form is *constituent*.

> *Nine players **constitute** a baseball team.*
>
> *The **constituent** parts of a business suit are a fitted jacket and matching pants.*

CORPUS

F. In your notebook, write sentences that tell the constituent parts of each of these things. Compare your answers with a partner.

1. a textbook
2. an orchestra
3. a computer
4. a burger

The verb *acquire* means "to obtain or gain something." You can acquire something physical (books, property, etc.) or abstract (knowledge, a skill, a habit, etc.).

> *I **acquired** an antique violin recently.*
>
> *I **acquired** a good education in my small-town school.*

The noun form is *acquisition*.

> *The violin is my most valuable **acquisition**.*
>
> *The **acquisition** of a second language is not easy.*

CORPUS

G. In your notebook, write a short paragraph about a real or imaginary trip that you took to a foreign country. Name at least four things that you acquired on your trip. Include the word *acquisition*. Be prepared to present your work in class.

H. Self-Assessment Review: Go back to page 49 and reassess your knowledge of the target vocabulary. How has your understanding of the words changed? What words do you feel most comfortable with now?

Writing and Discussion Topics

With a partner or small group, share ideas about the following topics. Then have each person write a paragraph about one of the topics.

1. What are some other groups of people (not described in this unit) that wear uniforms or special clothing? Describe what they wear and why.

2. Describe a special ceremony that you attended, such as a wedding or graduation. Describe who took part in the ceremony and what they wore. Were any symbols a part of the ceremony?

3. What are some reasons why sports teams wear uniforms?

UNIT 5

Success Story

In this unit, you will

> read about the meaning of success and what factors contribute to it.
> read about a personality trait related to success.
> review finding main ideas.
> increase your understanding of the target academic words for this unit.

READING SKILL Identifying Definitions

Self-Assessment

Think about how well you know each target word, and check (✓) the appropriate column. I have…

TARGET WORDS	never seen the word before	seen the word but am not sure what it means	seen the word and understand what it means	used the word, but am not sure if correctly	used the word confidently in *either* speaking *or* writing	used the word confidently in *both* speaking *and* writing
AWL						
attain						
🔑 aware						
coincide						
🔑 colleague						
🔑 demonstrate						
🔑 dominate						
dynamic						
exploit						
🔑 generate						
inhibit						
🔑 media						
🔑 positive						
🔑 professional						
🔑 role						

 🔑 Oxford 3000™ keywords

Outside the Reading What do you know about success?
Watch the video on the student website to find out more.

Before You Read

Read these questions. Discuss your answers in a small group.

1. How would you define success?

2. Are all famous people successful? Are all successful people famous? Give examples to support your opinion.

3. Name some people you consider successful. Why do you consider them successful?

Read

This article discusses important information about how to be successful. It defines success and explains what it takes to achieve it.

WHAT IS SUCCESS?

What is success? is it wealth? Fame? Power? We tend to think of success as something unusual, something that requires special talents to achieve. That's
5 because stories in the **media** about successful business executives, **professional** golfers, glamorous movie stars, best-selling authors, and powerful politicians lead us to believe that only a few special people are successful. We may
10 not hear about them, but ordinary people can be successful, too. Success is about reaching for something—and getting it. It is about having something you didn't have before. It is about **attaining** something that is valued by others.

Success requires ambition and hard work.

SETTING GOALS

15 Success begins with a clear goal, and **attaining** that goal requires ambition. Ambition is the energy that drives people to work hard, to learn more, and to seek opportunities to advance themselves. Some people have a clear goal, but they lack the ambition to make their dream come true. Other people have great ambition but no

20 clear goal to work toward. They start one scheme after another but never seem to find success.

THE NEED FOR PERSISTENCE

All children begin life with great ambition. Consider the ambition that babies **demonstrate** as they try to sit up, crawl, and walk. Despite repeated failures, they keep trying until they succeed.
25 What makes them keep trying? Persistence. This is the ability to focus on a task despite interruptions, obstacles, and setbacks. Persistence is strong throughout childhood. During the teen years, however, a fear of failure or a fear of being laughed at by

THE BUILDING BLOCKS OF SUCCESS

SUCCESS

CLEAR GOAL AMBITION

DYNAMIC PERSONALITY PERSISTENCE SUCCESSFUL PARENTS MIDDLE CLASS

others for trying to "be somebody" may **inhibit**, or stop, their
30 persistence. As a result, many teens seem to just quit trying.

THE ROLE OF PARENTS

If parents are **aware** that a lack of ambition is common in teenagers, they may be able to minimize it by providing **positive** learning experiences in the early years. For example, parents can encourage their young children to take on challenges, praise
35 them for trying, and comfort them if they fail. One of the strongest influences on a person's ambition is the family. It is not a **coincidence** that successful parents tend to raise successful children. However, is this due to heredity or upbringing? Evidence suggests that both play a **role** in
40 determining ambition.

THE ROLE OF ECONOMIC STATUS

The economic status of a family also influences a person's level of ambition. Young adults who grew up in poor families may be more focused on meeting the needs of today rather than reaching for the dreams of tomorrow. Or they may have great ambition but
45 lack the means to reach their goals. In contrast, ambition may be unnecessary for those who grew up in rich families because, at least financially, they are already successful. Not surprisingly, ambition seems to **coincide** most often with middle-class status.

Although financially secure, middle-class
50 families may not feel socially secure. This
status anxiety fuels the ambition needed to
reach for success.

THE ROLE OF PERSONALITY

Despite their backgrounds, it is people with
dynamic personalities who are most likely to
55 succeed. These are people who don't wait for
things to happen; these are people who take
effective action to <u>make</u> things happen. With
their eyes on the future, their goals **dominate**
the choices they make. They learn the skills they will need
60 through education or training. They **exploit**—that is, take
advantage of—opportunities to broaden their knowledge through
experience and observation. They seek assistance from anyone
who might further their chances to succeed, including family
members, friends, coaches, and **colleagues**.

ATTAINING SUCCESS

65 And finally success is very likely to happen for these **dynamic**
people. For each person it will be different, though, because
individuals **generate** their own definitions of success. So he or she
will get the job, win the race, earn the diploma, start the business,
or climb the mountain—and the goal will become a reality.

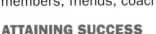
Each person has a different definition of success.

Reading Comprehension

A. Mark each sentence as *T* (True) or *F* (False) according to the information in Reading 1. Use your dictionary to check the meaning of new words.

___ 1. Stories generated by the media demonstrate that ordinary people can be successful.

___ 2. Family plays a major role in influencing a child's level of ambition.

___ 3. The teen years often coincide with a fear of failure and a lack of ambition.

___ 4. Positive learning experiences in the early years can inhibit persistence.

___ 5. Dynamic people are aware that they must take effective action to attain success.

___ 6. Despite their backgrounds, professional people are the most likely to succeed.

___ 7. Meeting the needs of today may dominate the thoughts of a young adult who grew up in a poor family.

___ 8. People seeking success might ask colleagues to assist them.

___ 9. One way to prepare for success is to exploit opportunities to learn through observation.

B. With a partner, decide which of these qualities contribute to success, according to Reading 1.

___ a clear goal   ___ middle-class status   ___ repeated failures

___ persistence   ___ focus   ___ a dynamic personality

___ a coincidence   ___ dreams of tomorrow   ___ successful parents

---

READING SKILL   Identifying Definitions

LEARN

The author of Reading 1 uses the entire passage to arrive at a full description of success. Each paragraph contains information that adds to the definition. Within the text, there are definitions of other words related to success. For some words, the author provides a definition; for example, *ambition* in paragraph 2. Other words are defined with a synonym; for example, *inhibit* in paragraph 3.

APPLY

Look back at Reading 1 to find definitions of these words. Write the definitions in your notebook.

1. ambition (paragraph 2)
2. persistence (paragraph 3)
3. inhibit (paragraph 3)
4. dynamic people (paragraph 6)
5. exploit (paragraph 6)

Vocabulary Activities   STEP I: Word Level

A. Use the target vocabulary in the box to complete this story. Use the words in parentheses to help you.

attained	dominant	positive
coincided with	dynamic	professional
demonstrated	generating	was aware

As a boy, Lance Armstrong excelled in many sports. By his teen years, however, bicycling had become the _____ interest in his life. He easily won
     (1. most important)

many local cycling races. But his goal was to be a _____ racer. In his
        (2. paid)

first race, he finished last of 111 riders. He was discouraged and almost quit racing.

Instead, he trained harder and soon _____ the rank of number one
     (3. reached)

bicyclist in the world. But his success _____ a terrible illness. Lance,
     (4. happened at the same time as)

just 25 years old, was diagnosed with advanced cancer. After long and painful

medical treatments, he was so weak that he again thought of quitting. He

_____ that he might never recover from his illness, but once more
     (5. knew)

this _____ young man _____ amazing persistence,
  (6. energetic)   (7. showed)

and he had a _____ attitude. He trained for two years, slowly
 (8. optimistic)

regaining strength and _____ a new goal: to compete in the Tour de
 (9. creating)

France bicycle race, one of the most demanding sports contests in the world. In

1999, Lance entered the Tour and won. He subsequently went on to win the Tour

seven years in a row.

Lance officially retired from cycling competitions in early 2011. He heads the

Lance Armstrong Foundation, which has raised millions of dollars for cancer research.

B. A *colleague* is a co-worker, someone you work with. With a partner, match the
worker in the left column with his or her colleague. Compare answers with
a partner. Writing in your notebooks, take turns making sentences with the
information.

_a_ 1. doctor   a. nurse

   *A doctor and a nurse are **colleagues**.*

___ 2. teacher   b. principal

___ 3. manicurist   c. publisher

___ 4. violinist   d. waiter

___ 5. chef   e. pianist

___ 6. author   f. hair stylist

In this unit, the word *role* is used to mean "the position of importance of
something."

   *Parents play a key **role** in the education of their children.*

   *Exercise plays a **role** in staying healthy. Diet plays a **role**, too.*

Role is also commonly used to refer to the part of a character in a film or play.

   *Several actors have played the **role** of Superman in films.*

CORPUS

C. Check (✓) the factors that play a role when teenagers quit trying to succeed,
according to Reading 1.

___ fear of challenge   ___ fear of being laughed at

___ lack of persistence   ___ lack of setbacks

___ fear of failure   ___ lack of experience

Now, with a partner, think of at least two other factors that may play a role. Discuss
your ideas in a small group.

The word *media* refers to the means of communication that reach many
people, such as television, radio, and newspapers. *Media* is a plural noun.
The singular form is *medium*, but this form is used less often. *Media* can also
be used as an adjective.

   *The news **media** cover national elections closely.*

   *National elections get a lot of **media** coverage.*

   *Some actors think that theater is a more satisfying **medium** than television.*

CORPUS

D. With a partner, classify these examples of media. Write *N* for news media, *P* for print media, *V* for visual media, and *A* for advertising media. More than one answer for each item is possible.

___ books   ___ magazines   ___ radio

___ the Internet   ___ newspapers   ___ television

E. To *generate* something means "to create, cause, or produce" it. What do these workers generate? Complete the sentences. Then, add one more sentence of your own about another worker. Compare answers with a partner.

1. A comedian generates _____ when people hear his jokes.

2. A saleswoman generates _____ for her company.

3. A computer programmer generates _____ for computers.

4. An architect generates _____ for new buildings.

5. _____ .

Vocabulary Activities   STEP II: Sentence Level

The verb *coincide* means "to happen at the same time as another event." It can also be used to refer to two ideas or opinions that agree.

> *The release of Disney's new film was scheduled to **coincide** with the first day of vacation.*

> *Voters could not re-elect a mayor whose views did not **coincide** with theirs.*

The noun form is *coincidence*. It refers to the surprising fact of two or more similar things happening at the same time by chance. The adjective form is *coincidental*.

> *By **coincidence**, Junko and Mariko came to the picnic wearing identical outfits.*

> *It was a **coincidence** that they had identical outfits.*

> *It was also **coincidental** that their husbands were wearing identical shirts.*

CORPUS

F. For each of these sets of sentences, circle the one sentence that describes a coincidence. Then, write a sentence in your notebook explaining what the coincidence is, using the word *coincidence* or *coincidental*.

1. a. Mr. Romano had spaghetti for lunch. His wife made spaghetti for dinner.

   b. Mr. and Mrs. Romano had spaghetti for dinner.

   *By **coincidence**, Mr. Romano had spaghetti for lunch on the same day that his wife made spaghetti for dinner.*

2. a. Dmitri got on a bus to go downtown. His friend Pavlo was on the same bus.

   b. Maria and Lupe got on a bus and they both went downtown to go to work.

3. a. Barry and Larry are twins. Their birthdays are on March 1.

   b. Sue and Lou are neighbors. Their birthdays are on June 1.

4. a. A family has five children. Each child's last name is Rodriguez.

   b. A basketball team has five players. Each player's last name is Rodriguez.

Word Form Chart			
Noun	**Verb**	**Adjective**	**Adverb**
dominance domination	dominate	dominant	_____

The verb *dominate* means "to have strong control over something" or "to be the most important part of something."

> My father **dominated** our lives when my brother and I were small.
>
> The huge brick fireplace **dominated** the living room.

 CORPUS

G. Complete this paragraph, using different forms of *dominate*. Compare your work with a partner.

The term "alpha male" is used in the science of animal behavior. It refers to the (1) _____ male in a group of animals, such as wolves. This term can also apply to people. Among humans, the alpha male tries to (2) _____ all of the other males in his social group; for example, his colleagues in the workplace. In the animal world, males may fight to attain (3) _____ over others. A human male may also "fight," but with words and actions that prove he is superior. Often the male who (4) _____ others is friendly and has clear goals, so others like having him as their leader.

To be *aware* means "to know about or realize something." The opposite is to be *unaware*. The noun form is *awareness*.

> Jon was **aware** that everyone was watching him.
>
> Jon had no **awareness** that his name was called.
>
> Jon seemed **unaware** of the audience's applause.

CORPUS

H. In your notebook, complete these sentences about successful people. Use your own ideas. Compare sentences with a partner.
1. A successful teacher is aware that . . .
2. During the race, marathon runners may be unaware that . . .
3. Someone who is applying for a job must be aware of . . .
4. To write a successful book, an author must have an awareness of . . .

Before You Read

Discuss your answers to these questions in a small group.

1. What is your definition of personality?

2. Do you know people who constantly talk about themselves? Why do you think they do that?

3. What are some things that famous people do that you don't approve of?

Read

This excerpt from a psychology textbook discusses a personality trait called narcissism and the characteristics of people with this type of personality.

I Love Me

N arcissus was the name of a character in an ancient Greek story. According to the story, he was very much in love with his own good looks. He drowned in a pool of water when he leaned over too far, to admire his handsome reflection. There is a personality trait named for Narcissus. It is called a
5 "narcissistic personality." People with this type of personality have great love for themselves, and this **coincides** with a strong need to be admired by others.

NARCISSISTIC BEHAVIOR

Most people who have a narcissistic personality are very ordinary people. However, they think of themselves as being very important and special. As a result, they often try to
10 **exploit** others. They expect other people to give them constant attention and to obey their commands. In a restaurant, for example, a narcissist might expect to be seated immediately. He might demand a better table, a special salad, or a sharper knife. Narcissists demand attention from
15 everyone, including their family, friends, **colleagues**, and even strangers.

On the other hand, narcissists can **demonstrate** great charm. They smile a lot. They gossip and tell jokes. They **generate** excitement with their lively chatter. They like to talk
20 about themselves and often **dominate** the conversation with stories about their **exploits**. In these stories they tend to greatly exaggerate their talents and personal **attainments**.

In fact, when narcissists describe their **attainments**, they are likely to be lying. Lying is typical behavior for narcissists, who often try to impress
25 people with false claims about things they own or people they know. They brag that their golf clubs are identical to the ones used by **professional**

golfers. They claim to be best friends with the mayor and the police chief and the bank president.

ROOTS OF NARCISSISM

This kind of talk seems to reflect great self-confidence
30 and self-esteem. However, psychologists suggest that this behavior results not from self-love, but actually from fear of failure and the subsequent shame it would bring. Some say that narcissism results if parents do not comfort young children when they
35 have been disappointed or have failed to **attain** something. The children view this as punishment and try to avoid future failure. As a result, they never learn to deal with disappointment or failure.

Narcissists can demonstrate great charm. They gossip and tell jokes.

Other psychologists have a slightly different theory. They believe that
40 a narcissistic personality arises when parents try to protect children from disappointment and failure by satisfying all of their demands. This **generates** in the children a lifelong pattern of expecting that they will always get what they want.

HOW NARCISSISTS SEE OTHERS

Narcissists do not see other people as human beings but rather as objects that
45 have no feelings or needs of their own. Narcissists believe that the **role** of other people is to satisfy their needs and to admire them. For this reason, narcissists seldom have truly close friends. Instead, they surround themselves with people they consider worthy of their greatness.

NARCISSISM IN CELEBRITIES

50 Oddly, the narcissistic traits that we find so annoying in ordinary people are the same traits that attract us to many entertainers and **professional** athletes. A recent study found that celebrities as a group are more narcissistic than other people. However, it is not fame
55 that makes celebrities narcissistic; it is the other way around. They were first narcissistic and were then drawn to careers that would earn them admiration from others.

Celebrities are often more narcissistic than other people.

They are very **aware** of the applause of their fans.
60 They see it as a **positive** message that they are loved and admired. But they may also **exploit** the **media** to get attention. For example, they wear show-off clothes and date gorgeous partners. They marry and divorce again and again. They buy expensive cars and drive too fast. Whatever they do, the **media** report it
65 because the **dynamic** personalities of the celebrities, and their apparent lack of **inhibitions**, seem exciting.

NARCISSISM IN ALL OF US

All of us have some narcissism, and that's good. Self-love is what motivates people to nourish and protect their bodies, to improve their minds, to learn new skills, and to discover the world in which they live. It is what gives
70 people the self-confidence to share a relationship with others and the ambition to reach for success. However, the self-love of those with a narcissistic personality type is so excessive that it overshadows everything else in their lives. ■

Reading Comprehension

Mark each sentence *T* (True) or *F* (False) according to the information in Reading 2. Use your dictionary to help you understand new words.

___ 1. Narcissists demand attention from everyone, including colleagues and strangers.

___ 2. A narcissist might try to exploit people because she believes she is very important.

___ 3. A narcissist is aware of other people's failures and demonstrates great concern.

___ 4. Narcissists often lie about what they have attained and dominate conversations with stories about themselves.

___ 5. Psychologists believe that narcissistic behavior coincides with self-esteem.

___ 6. Psychologists believe that parents play a role in generating narcissism in their children.

___ 7. Celebrities get attention from the media because their behavior makes them seem uninhibited.

___ 8. Professional athletes become narcissistic as a result of their careers.

READING SKILL   Identifying Definitions

APPLY

A. Complete these sentences to define the characteristics of narcissists. Refer to Reading 2 for information.

1. They think of themselves as being _____ .

2. They often try _____ .

3. They expect other people to _____ .

4. They demand _____ from _____ .

5. They can demonstrate _____ .

6. They like to _____ .

7. They often dominate _____ .

8. They tend to exaggerate _____ .

9. _____ is typical behavior.

10. They believe that the role of other people is _____ .

11. Their self-love overshadows _____ .

B. Write a definition of *narcissism* in your own words.

REVIEW A SKILL **Finding the Main Idea** (See p. 21)

In your own words, state the main idea of Reading 1 and of Reading 2.

Vocabulary Activities STEP I: Word Level

In this unit, the adjective *professional* is used to describe activities for which participants are paid. *A professional* (noun) is someone who is paid for his or her work. The adverb form is *professionally*.

> College sports dominate TV time on Saturdays and **professional** sports dominate on Sundays.

> Those artists are **professionals**. I'm just an amateur.

> Her real name is Mary Jones, but she's known **professionally** as Lucille Fontaine.

CORPUS

A. Work with a partner. Write *P* for each activity that is done only by professionals. Write *A* for each activity that is done for fun, only by amateurs. Write *B* for each activity that could be done by both professionals and amateurs.

___ 1. fishing   ___ 4. playing basketball   ___ 7. taking photographs

___ 2. designing airplanes   ___ 5. watching television   ___ 8. cooking

___ 3. skiing   ___ 6. exercising   ___ 9. performing surgery

A *dynamic* person is someone who is effective and active. He or she is full of ideas and energy.

> **Dynamic** people make good leaders.

Dynamic can also be used to refer to a force or energy that causes change in people or events.

> The dairy industry has had to adapt to **dynamic** market conditions.

CORPUS

B. With a partner, check (✓) the jobs that could best be done by a dynamic person. Explain your choices.

___ farmer   ___ mail carrier   ___ salesperson

___ film actor   ___ politician   ___ teacher

___ gardener   ___ receptionist   ___ wedding planner

Now, with your partner, complete these sentences with the names of inventions that have had a dynamic influence. (More than one answer is possible.)

1. _____ had a dynamic influence on the way people cook.
2. _____ had a dynamic influence on overseas travel.
3. _____ had a dynamic influence on preventing illness.

The central meaning of the adjective *positive* is "yes." It has many uses:

good, helpful, or useful	*The new law had a **positive** effect on the economy.* *Thank you for your **positive** suggestions.*
accepting or approving	*The audience had a **positive** reaction to the new play.*
hopeful	*A **positive** attitude is important if you want to reach your goals.*
certain or confident	*I'm **positive** that Cairo is the capital of Egypt.*
affirming	*The blood test was **positive**. She has malaria.*

CORPUS

C. With a partner, decide which meaning of *positive* is used in each sentence.

1. If parents are aware that a lack of ambition is common in teenagers, they may be able to minimize it by providing positive learning experiences in the early years.

2. Entertainers believe that the applause of their fans is a positive message that they are loved and admired.

3. The metal detector that screens air travelers gave a positive reading.

To *attain* something means "to succeed in achieving a goal, usually after great effort." Be careful not to confuse "attain" with "obtain," which means "to get something."

> *Dr. Arnet **attained** the rank of professor. Then, he obtained a new desk for his office.*
>
> *I see now that being an opera singer is not an **attainable** goal.*

CORPUS

D. Complete these sentences, using *obtained* or *attained*.

1. Frank Brown _____ a driver's license.
2. Li Xiao Ping _____ an Olympic gold medal.
3. Admiral Blanc _____ the rank of a Naval Commander.
4. Abdullah _____ tickets for tomorrow's basketball game.

Now, with a partner, decide which of these things are attainable by most people. Which are unattainable? Write *A* for attainable and *U* for unattainable. Discuss your answers in a small group.

___ a high school diploma   ___ an Olympic gold medal

___ a journey to the moon   ___ fluency in a second language

___ a Nobel prize   ___ happiness

___ a well-paying job   ___ the starring role in a film

The verb *exploit* has the general meaning of "use," but can express two different ideas. It's important to understand which idea is being expressed in a particular sentence.

use something cleverly or productively	*A good student* **exploits** *every opportunity to read outside of class.*
use something unfairly or selfishly	*Some companies* **exploit** *workers by not paying them a fair salary.*

The noun form, *exploitation,* almost always has the second, negative meaning.

> *The* **exploitation** *of workers is unfair.*

E. Work with a partner. Write *P* for the sentences that use *exploit* in a positive way. Write *N* for the sentences that use the word in a negative way.

___ 1. Some parents exploit their children by pushing them to perform in movies or TV shows.

___ 2. He exploited every chance to improve his writing skills.

___ 3. She exploited her friends by borrowing money every day.

___ 4. He exploited his musical talent by playing with a band.

In this unit, *demonstrate* means "to prove or show something." A *demonstrative* person shows his or her feelings very clearly.

> *Her paintings* **demonstrate** *a great love of her country.*

> *My little granddaughter is so* **demonstrative**. *She is always hugging me.*

Another common meaning is "to give directions about how something is done."

> *My trainer* **demonstrated** *how to use the new exercise bicycle.*

To *demonstrate* is also often used to mean "to publicly show your support for or against a social or political cause."

> *A group was* **demonstrating** *in front of city hall yesterday.*

> *Fifty* **demonstrators** *took part in a* **demonstration** *against high taxes.*

F. Complete this paragraph, using different forms of *demonstrate*. Compare your work with a partner.

Although most narcissists live ordinary lives, it is possible for a narcissist to become the coach of a professional athletic team. What a great way to (1) _____ his or her importance. These coaches (2) _____ their power by demanding absolute obedience from their players. They may order punishment for any (3) _____ of disobedience. If a player (4) _____ any behavior that could destroy team unity, the coach may remove him or her from the team.

To *inhibit* an action means "to stop it or to decrease it."

> *Fear of failure **inhibited** him from participating in the race.*
> *Antibiotics **inhibit** the growth of bacteria.*

The noun form, *inhibition*, refers to the feeling of embarrassment or fear that stops someone from speaking freely or acting freely. The adjective forms are *inhibited* and *uninhibited*.

> *Most actors don't mind acting silly because they are **uninhibited**. They have no **inhibitions**. Most other adults have a hard time acting silly. They are too **inhibited**.*

 CORPUS

G. Read this story. Then, in your notebook, rewrite the sentences using different forms of *inhibit*. Be prepared to read your sentences aloud or discuss them in a small group.

1. Last year, Ahn went to Canada because the economic slowdown in his home country reduced his professional opportunities.

2. Adjusting to a new country was hard. He was too shy to make friends with his colleagues. He worried that his English was poor.

3. He wanted to feel more free when he spoke, so Ahn decided to join an English class.

4. His teacher told the students, "Try to lose your shyness and negative feelings. It's okay to make mistakes."

5. The teacher understood why the students were embarrassed. He made them feel more comfortable, and soon the students were laughing and talking, learning English, and making friends.

H. Self-Assessment Review: Go back to page 65 and reassess your knowledge of the target vocabulary. How has your understanding of the words changed? What words do you feel most comfortable with now?

With a partner, share ideas about each of the following topics. Then have each person write a paragraph about one of the topics.

1. Imagine you would like to work as a salesperson. What qualities are important for someone in this position? What would you say about yourself that would be truthful yet emphasize your positive qualities? Write a letter to an imaginary company that describes your qualities and asks about job opportunities.

2. Can a narcissistic person also be a successful person? What qualities do narcissistic people have that might help them be successful? What qualities might inhibit their success?

3. Sir Winston Churchill said this about success: "Success is the ability to go from one failure to another with no loss of enthusiasm." Do you agree or disagree? Give an example to support your opinion.

Solving Crimes with Science

In this unit, you will

> read about the use of science to solve crimes.
> review identifying examples.
> increase your understanding of the target academic words for this unit.

READING SKILL Identifying Time and Sequence Words

Self-Assessment

Think about how well you know each target word, and check (✓) the appropriate column. I have…

TARGET WORDS	never seen the word before	seen the word but am not sure what it means	seen the word and understand what it means	used the word, but am not sure if correctly	used the word confidently in *either* speaking *or* writing	used the word confidently in *both* speaking *and* writing
AWL						
🔑 authority						
🔑 conclude						
🔑 consult						
contrary						
detect						
🔑 establish						
🔑 instance						
🔑 logic						
motive						
🔑 panel						
🔑 site						
🔑 specific						
🔑 tape						
🔑 technical						

🔑 Oxford 3000™ keywords

 Outside the Reading What do you know about science?
Watch the video on the student website to find out more.

Before You Read

Read these questions. Discuss your answers in a small group.

1. Do you ever watch crime stories on television? If so, which one is your favorite?

2. Why do you think people like movies, TV programs, or books about solving crimes?

3. What are some ways that science can help the police solve crimes?

🔊 Read

This chapter from a book of true crime stories tells how the police solved a case of theft.

Solving a Crime with Science: A True Story

It was 7:30 in the evening. Millionaire Eduard Arellano and his wife Susan were late. They had tickets for a play at a nearby theater, so they were rushing to leave the house. They set the security alarm, locked the front door of their 16-room mansion, and sped away in their BMW.

5   A tall man watched them drive off. He removed a key from a red cloth bag that he carried and used it to unlock the front door. Once inside, he turned off the security alarm.

The tall man knew that Eduard and Susan would be gone for hours. He would have plenty of time to do his job. He went directly to an upstairs
10 bedroom. He pushed open a wall **panel** and used a code to open a hidden safe. Inside the safe were trays of sparkling rings, necklaces, and earrings.

As soon as Eduard and Susan arrived at the theater, they realized that they had
15 forgotten the tickets. Susan insisted that they return home to get them. When they arrived home, she was surprised to find the front door unlocked and the alarm system turned off. "Someone has been
20 in here," Susan **concluded**. "I'm calling the police." She was told that a police **detective** would be at the **site** in a few minutes.

When the tall man heard voices downstairs, he knew he had to leave at
25 once. He quickly stuffed the jewelry into the red bag. Then he opened a
window and climbed down to a flat roof. From there he jumped to the grass
and ran off.

Minutes later, the police **detective** and a team of crime scene investigators
(CSI) arrived. The **detective** searched the house. Only one room showed signs
30 of a crime. In an upstairs bedroom he found an open window and an empty
safe, but no thief. He **consulted** Eduard and Susan, but only the jewelry
seemed to be missing.

The **detective** was puzzled. At other **sites,** a
thief opened nearly every drawer in the house
35 searching for valuables. To the **contrary**, this thief
seemed to know exactly where to find valuables.
He also knew how to unlock the front door and
open the safe. It seemed **logical** that the thief
knew the house. The **detective** asked Eduard and
40 Susan many questions. He asked about their
servant. He wanted to know the **specific** time
they had returned home. Could Eduard and Susan
be lying? What **motive** would they have for faking
a theft? Could the servant be guilty?

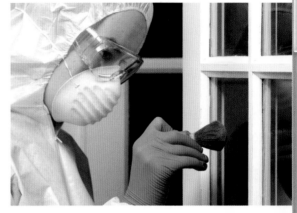

45 Meanwhile, the CSIs were upstairs checking the bedroom for fingerprints
and searching for evidence—signs that might help solve the crime. They found
a button by the open window, and they **detected** a tiny red thread near the
safe. They put these pieces of evidence into envelopes and **taped** them shut.
Then they searched the garden.

50 The next day, the **detective** drove to the home of the servant. There in a
trash bin the **detective** found a grass-stained shirt with a button missing. In a
closet he found a red cloth bag—but no jewelry.
The servant was arrested and taken to the police
station, where he was fingerprinted.

55 Subsequent tests done at a police laboratory
established that the grass stains on the shirt
matched the type of grass at the mansion. The
button came from the same shirt. Lab tests
further **established** that the red thread matched
60 the cloth of the red bag. And the servant's
fingerprints matched fingerprints from the crime
site. In each **instance**, the evidence pointed to
the servant's guilt.

Authorities accused the servant of theft, and
65 he confessed to the crime. He described where he had hidden the jewelry. He
said that he was **motivated** to steal because he needed money. He added,
however, that Mr. Arellano had told him how to do it. Mr. Arellano said they
could both make money. The servant could sell the jewelry and Eduard could
be paid for his losses by his insurance company.

70 At a court trial, the servant was found guilty and sentenced to five years in
prison. **Technically**, Eduard was guilty, too, and he was sentenced to prison
for his role in the crime. Good **detective** work and modern science helped
solve a crime. ■

Reading Comprehension

Mark each sentence as *T* (True) or *F* (False) according to the information in Reading 1.
Use your dictionary to check the meaning of new words.

___ 1. Contrary to what Susan expected, the front door was unlocked and the alarm was turned off. She concluded that someone was inside.

___ 2. A detective asked Eduard and Susan many questions. For instance, he asked about the specific time they left the house.

___ 3. It seemed logical to the detective that the thief knew the house.

___ 4. Technically, Eduard and the servant were both guilty of a crime.

___ 5. The thief found money in a hidden wall panel.

___ 6. CSIs put the jewelry in an envelope and taped it shut.

___ 7. The detective consulted with Susan and Eduard about the shirt that the CSIs found at the crime site.

___ 8. The crime lab established that the red thread matched the cloth of the red bag.

___ 9. Authorities accused the servant of theft. His motive was to make money.

READING SKILL   Identifying Time and Sequence Words

LEARN

Understanding the *order of events* in a story is often essential for understanding the story, especially a mystery such as Reading 1. The order of events can be shown in several ways:

1. Sentences in a paragraph usually describe actions in the order that they happened.

2. Time words such as *Monday, March, summer,* or *1989* tell when actions took place.

3. Words such as *before, after, soon, first, next, meanwhile, then, finally,* and *subsequently* can show the order of events.

4. Phrases such as *three days later, the next year,* and *at the same time* also show time order.

APPLY

A. With a partner, use time clues and logic to figure out the order in which these events in Reading 1 took place. Number them from *1* to *9*.

___ A detective arrives.

___ The tall man hears voices downstairs.

___ Susan calls the police.

___ Susan realizes they have forgotten their tickets.

___ The tall man watches Susan and Eduard drive off.

___ Eduard tells the servant how to open the safe.

___ The tall man stuffs the jewelry into the red bag.

___ Susan concludes that someone is inside.

___ The tall man climbs out of the window.

B. For each sentence, decide which action happened first and which happened second. Mark them *1* and *2*.

___ They realized that they had forgotten the tickets
___ as soon as they arrived at the theater.

___ They were surprised to find the front door unlocked
___ when they arrived home.

___ He knew he had to leave
___ when he heard voices downstairs.

___ He climbed out of the window
___ after emptying the safe.

___ He waited for them to drive away
___ before unlocking the door.

Vocabulary Activities   STEP I: Word Level

The verb *consult* means "to ask somebody for information" or "to seek information in a book or other reference."

> The police **consulted** a doctor to learn about the effects of the drug.
>
> I **consulted** my calendar to see when my dentist appointment was.

CORPUS

A. With a partner, decide whom or what you would consult for information about each of these things.

1. the meaning of a word
2. a recipe for chicken soup
3. the price of an airplane ticket to London
4. the telephone number of a restaurant

B. Use the target vocabulary in the box to complete this story. Use the words in parentheses to help you.

conclude	detect	logic
consult	establish	site
contrary	instance	specific

Sherlock Holmes is a fictional detective, created by Sir Arthur Conan Doyle about a hundred years ago. Readers learn that Holmes is known for using

_____ and observation to solve crimes. As a result, the police
(1. reasoning)

_____ him when they have a difficult case. In each
(2. ask advice from)

_____ , Holmes carefully examines the crime _____
(3. event)   (4. location)

for evidence. He might _____ faint footprints that the police
(5. notice)

overlooked. He might find a broken clock that can _____ the
(6. tell)

_____ time the crime was committed. He often discusses the
(7. exact)
evidence with his friend, Dr. Watson. Usually Watson reasons incorrectly. He
might say, "Then I must _____ that the husband did it." "On
(8. decide)
the _____ , my dear Watson," Holmes might reply. "It was her
(9. opposite)
jealous sister."

A *site* is a location or a place where an event has happened or will happen.

> Police were called to the **site** of the accident.

A *website* is a location on the Internet.

> The university's **website** listed all of the faculty members.

> The **site** didn't list their office hours, though.

CORPUS

C. With a partner, match the sites on the left with the people who might go to that site on the right. Discuss the reasons why the people go to the sites.

___ 1. accident site   a. a rock band

___ 2. construction site   b. a bride and groom

___ 3. battle site   c. an emergency medical team

___ 4. wedding site   d. students

___ 5. concert site   e. carpenters

___ 6. graduation site   f. soldiers

The word *contrary* is most commonly used in an expression that shows disagreement.

> Nayef: It's too hot today.

> Ahmed: On the **contrary**, it's just right.

It is also used to show an opposite action.

> **Contrary** to my parents' advice, I decided to become a lawyer.

CORPUS

D. Imagine that two people witnessed a man stealing a cell phone. They disagree when they talk to the police about what happened. With a partner, complete this conversation. Use *on the contrary*.

First Person	**Second Person**
1. The robber was really tall.	On the contrary, he was short.
2. He was wearing a black coat.	On the contrary, . . .
3. He looked very young to me.	
4. He was with a friend.	
5. He said, "I need a cell phone."	
6. He looked scared.	
7. He got on a bus at the corner.	

A *motive* is a reason for an action. The word is often used, as it is in this unit, to refer to the reason someone commits a crime.

> *Jim needed money fast. That was his* **motive** *for robbing the store.*

There are other, equally common usages of *motive* and its forms. The verb *motivate* means "to cause someone to act in a particular way," or "to make someone want to do something."

> *Desire to attend the music academy* **motivated** *her to practice every day.*

> *The promise of a raise can* **motivate** *employees to work harder.*

The noun form is *motivation.* It refers to the reason for doing something, or a positive feeling about doing something.

> *The employees showed a lot of* **motivation** *and finished the project quickly.*

Someone who feels eager to do something is *motivated.* Someone who does not feel eager to do something is *unmotivated.*

> *Despite interesting lessons and good teachers, some kids remain* **unmotivated**.

CORPUS

E. Write one or more sentences in your notebook according to the directions. Share your sentences with a small group.

1. Teachers can motivate their students in many ways. Describe how a teacher once motivated you.

2. Describe how advertisements can motivate people to do something.

3. Some people seem to always act kind (or mean). Describe what their motive might be for acting kind (or mean).

Establish is commonly used to mean "to start something," like "establish a new school." In the context of this unit, however, *establish* is used to mean "to learn facts that prove something is true."

> *Detectives* **established** *that the murdered man owed money to many people.*

CORPUS

F. In your notebook, write sentences that answer the questions. Use a form of *establish* in each sentence. Refer to Reading 1 for information.

1. What did the detective find out when he searched the house?

2. What did the tall man learn when he watched Eduard and Susan drive away?

3. What did Susan learn when she tried to open the door to get the tickets?

4. What did the laboratory tests show about the servant's fingerprints?

The adjective *specific* means "detailed" or "exact." It can also be used to refer to something particular rather than general. The adverb form is *specifically*. The verb form is *specify*. *The specifics* is a phrase that means "facts" or "details."

> *The newspaper reporter wanted to know the **specifics** of the crime.*

CORPUS

G. **Read these sentences about what the police do after a crime has occurred. Rewrite the sentences in your notebook, using the form of *specific* in parentheses.**

1. The police ask many definite questions, like the victim's name and age. (*specific*)

2. They need to know what happened. (*specifics*)

3. They want to know the details about when the crime happened. (*specifically*)

4. They want witnesses to tell exactly what they saw. (*specify*)

5. They hope witnesses can give them particular information about the crime. (*specific*)

The noun *logic* refers to the use of reasoning to decide if something is possible or correct.

> *Instead of using **logic** to solve the puzzle, he tried guessing.*

A *logical* decision or idea is reasonable and sensible. A decision that is based on guessing, feelings, or unreasonable conclusions is *illogical*.

> *It did not seem **logical** that a man would buy a car and then sell it the next day.*
>
> *It seemed **illogical** for him to buy a car one day and sell it the next.*

CORPUS

H. **Read this story. Then, in your notebook, write five sentences about the facts in the story. Use forms of *establish*, *logical*, and *motive*. Be prepared to read aloud or discuss your sentences in a small group.**

Mr. Able, a jewelry store owner, claims he was robbed of $1 million in jewels. He sued his insurance company when the company refused to pay him for the loss. Mr. Able said that one rainy winter day, a robber ran into the store carrying a gun and an umbrella. The robber kept the gun pointed at Mr. Able as he tied up his hands. Then the robber opened the safe in the back room and took all 536 pieces of jewelry. He stuffed them into a suitcase and ran out the door.

The insurance company's lawyer had a contrary point of view. He concluded that the details of Mr. Able's story are technically impossible. The lawyer said that the tape in the store's surveillance camera would show what really happened and prove that Mr. Able was lying. The tape shows the robber entering the store wearing a raincoat and carrying an umbrella—but they are not wet. He is not carrying a suitcase. The tape shows Mr. Able helping the robber tie his hands. The robber disappears into a back room for just 14 seconds, and then leaves the store carrying a suitcase. The suitcase is too small to hold 536 pieces of jewelry. The robber leaves nearly $20,000 cash in the safe. The lawyer claimed that a friend pretended to rob Mr. Able for a share of the insurance money. His reason—he wanted to get rich quick.

Before You Read

Read these questions. Discuss your answers in a small group.

1. What does a detective do?

2. How can a science laboratory be used to help solve a crime?

3. Is it possible for someone to commit a "perfect" crime that leaves no clues? Why or why not?

Read

This online magazine article discusses the role of scientific laboratory analysis in helping the police solve crimes.

FORENSIC SCIENCE

Actor Basil Rathbone as Sherlock Holmes

Sherlock Holmes, a fictional **detective** of a century ago, was one of the first to use forensic science—the scientific analysis of physical evidence
5 to solve crimes. Holding a big magnifying glass, Holmes inspected crime scenes for footprints, broken glass, hair—anything that might help identify the person who committed the crime. In today's world, Holmes might be
10 a CSI, or crime scene investigator.

Today, when a crime is reported—a murder, for **instance**—the police immediately send a medical examiner (ME) and a CSI team to the crime **site**. The ME and CSIs will be part of a **panel** of **technical** experts in the investigation.

MES AND CSIS

15 At the crime scene, the ME examines the body of the victim and looks for wounds or marks that might be related to the crime. The ME also takes many photographs of the body. The body is subsequently taken away for a detailed examination that will **establish** the cause and time of the victim's death.

20 Meanwhile, CSIs first take hundreds of photographs of the crime **site**. Next they check the **site** for fingerprints. Most fingerprints form when sweat or another oily substance on a fingertip leaves an invisible imprint on a glass, tabletop, or other object. CSIs dust a black powder on objects at the crime **site** to make these
25 prints visible. The CSIs then look for drops of blood, strands of hair, pieces of ripped cloth, or other evidence that might link someone to the crime **site**.

FINDING TRACE EVIDENCE

"Every contact leaves a trace," according to an **authority** in forensics. This means that whenever a crime involves physical
30 contact, the criminal either leaves something at the **site**, takes something from the **site,** or both. This might be any number of substances, including hair, animal fur, sand, grass, and fibers from clothing or carpeting. Such trace evidence is usually difficult to **detect**, so, like Sherlock Holmes, CSIs rely on handheld
35 magnifying glasses to examine the crime scene. CSIs might even vacuum the entire area to collect tiny samples. They carefully label each piece of evidence as they collect it.

THE FORENSICS LABORATORY

The collected evidence is then sent to a forensics laboratory. There, forensic scientists will analyze it to **establish** how and when the
40 murder took place, where it took place, and who did it. Sometimes the evidence will even show *why* it took place; that is, the **motive** for the killing.

Among all the evidence found at the **site**, fingerprints are **conclusive.** This is because no two people have the
45 same fingerprints. Fingerprints from a crime scene are analyzed by computer to determine if they match the prints of a known criminal or crime suspect—a person who might be guilty of a crime.

DNA is another **conclusive** means of identification because
50 each person's DNA is unique. DNA is contained in cells of the body, so that evidence of hair, blood, tears, sweat, or other bodily fluids found at a crime scene can be used to link a **specific** person to the crime. Like fingerprints, DNA samples are analyzed by computer to determine if they
55 match the DNA of a known criminal or a suspect.

Voices, too, are unique. Samples of voices from security camera **tapes**, telephone answering machines, or other recording devices can be scanned electronically. A printout of the scan will show patterns of highs and lows, rhythm, and volume that can be
60 compared to patterns of a suspect's voice. However, **authorities** have **contrary** opinions about using voiceprints for identification.

Some argue that voices can change over time as people age or suffer illnesses, so old voiceprints are not always reliable.

In the laboratory, forensic scientists use an electron microscope
65 to scan samples of the substances that were collected at the crime scene. Then they enlarge the samples (up to 150,000×) on a visual display unit. This allows them to easily compare those samples with samples found at another location or on a suspect's clothing.

70 Forensic laboratories have on file the shoe print patterns of thousands of kinds of shoes. These can be compared to shoeprints found at a crime scene to **establish** the size and kind of shoes worn by a suspect. If the shoeprint was made in a soft
75 material, like mud, the lab may be able to tell the height and weight of the person by the depth of each step and the distance between steps.

After all of the evidence has been analyzed, the police chief **consults** with **panel** members. Based on the evidence, they
80 determine if it is **logical** to accuse and arrest a crime suspect. If it is, members of the **panel** may later be asked to present their forensic evidence in a court of law as proof of a suspect's guilt.

Reading Comprehension

Mark each sentence as *T* (True) or *F* (False) according to the information in Reading 2.
Use your dictionary to check the meaning of new words.

___ 1. Holmes inspected a crime site for anything related to the crime; for instance, footprints, broken glass, or hair.

___ 2. CSIs are part of a panel of technical experts in a forensic investigation.

___ 3. Forensic laboratories establish when and where a murder took place by taking hundreds of photographs.

___ 4. To identify footprints, forensic laboratories consult files of footprints of known criminals.

___ 5. CSIs use handheld magnifying glasses to detect trace evidence at crime scenes.

___ 6. Authorities have contrary opinions about using fingerprints for identification.

___ 7. DNA analysis can conclusively establish the motive for a crime.

___ 8. Samples of a suspect's voice can be compared to voice samples from surveillance tapes or telephone answering machines.

___ 9. A suspect will be arrested if, based on the evidence, it seems logical that he or she committed the crime.

___10. Fingerprints found at a crime scene can be linked to a specific individual if they match the individual's fingerprints.

APPLY

A. Scan the first four paragraphs of Reading 2. Answer the questions in complete sentences. Include the time words or phrases used in the Reading.

1. When did Sherlock Holmes do his detective work?

   _____

2. When do the police send an ME and a CSI team?

   _____

3. When do the CSIs take photographs in relation to other tasks?

   _____

B. Number these tasks from *1* to *7*, in the order in which they are done by the CSI team.

___ dust objects for fingerprints

___ take photographs

___ send evidence to a forensics laboratory

___ present their evidence in a court of law

___ look for drops of blood or strands of hair

___ label the evidence

___ consult with the police chief

REVIEW A SKILL Identifying Examples (See pp. 52–53)

What kind of examples are listed in paragraph 4?

_____

What kind of examples are listed in paragraph 5?

_____

Vocabulary Activities STEP I: Word Level

The adjective *technical* refers to the knowledge of machines, materials, and processes used in science and industry.

> Forensic scientists use their **technical** skills to analyze crime scene evidence.

This unit also uses the adverb *technically*, which means "according to an exact interpretation of a law or a fact."

> You can't come in yet. It's only 9:58. **Technically**, the store doesn't open until 10:00.

Another common use of the word *technical* is to refer to words and concepts related to a particular subject.

> "Stress" is a **technical** word used in engineering.

CORPUS

A. Complete the story with the words from the box.

technical assistance	technical person	logic	site
technical explanation	technical words		

My computer printer wasn't working right, so I called the company hotline for

(1) _____ _____ . The guy on the phone gave me a

(2) _____ _____ of the problem. I said, "Stop!

You're using too many (3) _____ _____ . I'm not a

(4) _____ _____ ."

So he said, "See the button that says ON? Just push that."

B. With a partner, complete these sentences with your own ideas. Share your ideas with the class.
1. "I know your 21st birthday is tomorrow, but today you are technically…"
2. "The sign says three lemons for one dollar. Technically, one lemon would cost…"
3. "Waiter, a fly fell into my soup." "I'm sorry, but the restaurant is not technically responsible for…"
4. "I see the sign that says No Parking, but technically I'm not parked, I'm just…"

C. With a partner, decide who has the authority to punish someone who breaks the rules or laws in these situations.
1. in a soccer game 3. in a city 5. in an office
2. in a classroom 4. in a family 6. in a store

An *authority* is a recognized expert in a field. The adjective form is *authoritative*.

> Professor West is an **authority** on the history of crime.

> He wrote an **authoritative** book titled Crime in Nineteenth Century Britain.

An *authority* is also a person or group that has the power to make rules or laws.

> The city transportation **authority** wants the bus company to add new routes.

Authority (noncount noun) refers to the power that such a person or group has.

> Parental **authority** today is not as strong as it was in the past.

CORPUS

D. When police detectives need special information to solve a crime, they consult an *authority*. With a partner, match the authorities on the left with their areas of special knowledge. Take turns making sentences with the information. Look up unfamiliar words in your dictionary.

_a_ 1. ornithologist   a. birds

*An ornithologist is an **authority** on birds.*

___ 2. zoologist   b. weather

___ 3. graphologist   c. animals

___ 4. toxicologist   d. handwriting

___ 5. meteorologist   e. poisons

Vocabulary Activities | STEP II: Sentence Level

Word Form Chart			
Noun	**Verb**	**Adjective**	**Adverb**
detective detection detector	detect	detectable	_____

E. Complete this paragraph by using a form of *detect* in each blank. Compare work with a partner.

A polygraph is a machine that is often called a "lie (1) _____ ." It is used by some (2) _____ when they question suspects. The polygraph is based on the belief that, if a person is lying, his or her body will react with (3) _____ physical changes, such as increased blood pressure and heart rate. The machine (4) _____ these changes and records them. If the polygraph shows that physical changes occurred when the suspect answered, the (5) _____ concludes that the suspect is lying. However, polygraph tests are only 70–90% accurate. This means that 10–30% of those tested might escape (6) _____ even if they are guilty—or they might be considered guilty even though they are innocent.

An *instance* is an example or case of a particular kind of occurrence.

*Yesterday's bank robbery was another **instance** of crime in the neighborhood.*

For instance is a common phrase that means, "for example."

*Bank security was poor. **For instance**, the cashiers had no warning alarms.*

CORPUS

F. Match each sentence on the right with the example that goes with it on the left. Use *for instance* to join the sentences, and write them in your notebook. Compare answers with a partner.

*Bank security was poor. **For instance**, there was no guard at the door.*

<u>d</u> 1. Bank security was poor.

___ 2. The robbers were armed.

___ 3. The robbers didn't plan very well.

___ 4. The robbers covered their faces.

___ 5. The robbers did not seem very smart.

a. one was wearing a black ski mask.

b. none had a specific job to do.

c. each robber had a gun or a knife.

d. there was no guard at the door.

e. the note said GIV ME YOR MONEE.

The verb *conclude* has the general meaning of "end" or "finish." It can also mean "to reach a decision after thought or study." The adjective *conclusive* refers to something that is definitely true.

*The lawyer **concluded** his summation of the case and calmly sat down.*

*The jury **concluded** that the suspect was guilty.*

*His fingerprint on the knife is **conclusive** proof that he is guilty.*

The noun form is *conclusion*. It is used in some common expressions:

reach a **conclusion**   make a judgment after careful consideration
come to a **conclusion**   make a decision after careful consideration
jump to **conclusions**   make a judgment based on feelings, not facts

 CORPUS

G. Read these statements about a crime. In your notebook, answer each question that follows, using a form of *conclude*. Be prepared to read aloud and explain your answers in a small group.

> • A valuable painting was stolen from a popular art museum.
> • Jim's fingerprints were found on the wall where the painting had been.
> • Jim said he didn't steal the painting. A polygraph test showed that he was not lying.
> • His friend, Dave, said that Jim was with him at the time the theft took place.
> • The painting was found in Dave's house. It had Dave's fingerprints on it.

1. Who did the police decide was guilty?

2. What did the police decide about the fingerprints on the wall? Why?

3. What evidence proved who was guilty?

H. Imagine that you are Hosun Kim, a private detective (rather than a police detective). You help companies solve problems. You have just received an email offering you a job. After you investigate Ms. Park, write in your notebook an "email" to Mr. Lee telling him what you found. Include forms of the words *detect*, *consult*, *motive*, and *conclude*. Share your email with a partner or small group.

Dear Mr. Kim,

I am in charge of medical claims for the ABC Insurance Company. We have an unusual case and want to hire you to help us.

Ms. Jenny Park has requested payment of $500,000. She says that she cannot walk and that she is unable to work. She says she had to hire someone to take care of her children and to do other domestic jobs. We are certain that she is perfectly healthy. Please investigate her situation for us. We will pay for your time and your expenses to prove that she should not be paid $500,000.

Sincerely,
Jack Lee
Chief Claims Investigator for ABC Insurance

I. Self-Assessment Review: Go back to page 81 and reassess your knowledge of the target vocabulary. How has your understanding of the words changed? What words do you feel most comfortable with now?

Writing and Discussion Topics

With a partner or small group, share ideas about the following topics. Then have each person write a paragraph about one of the topics.

1. Find an article in a newspaper or news magazine that describes a crime. Describe what happened.

2. What qualities should a good police detective have? Why?

3. In some countries, the media are given access to information about crimes as the specifics become available. In other countries, the media may not publish or broadcast information about a crime investigation. Which do you think is the better way? Why?

UNIT 7

BUSINESS

The Fast-Food Revolution

In this unit, you will

> read about the fast food revolution and the subsequent expansion of franchises.
> review identifying examples.
> increase your understanding of the target academic words for this unit.

READING SKILL Reading Numerical Tables

Self-Assessment

Think about how well you know each target word, and check (✓) the appropriate column. I have…

TARGET WORDS	never seen the word before	seen the word but am not sure what it means	seen the word and understand what it means	used the word, but am not sure if correctly	used the word confidently in *either* speaking *or* writing	used the word confidently in *both* speaking *and* writing
AWL						
🔑 abandon						
🔑 acknowledge						
albeit						
complement						
🔑 contemporary						
🔑 contrast						
🔑 decade						
🔑 economy						
🔑 expand						
🔑 generation						
🔑 grade						
incline						
🔑 output						
overlap						
🔑 reject						

🔑 Oxford 3000™ keywords

 Outside the Reading What do you know about business?
Watch the video on the student website to find out more.

97

Before You Read

Read these questions. Discuss your answers in a small group.

1. Think about the last time you ate in a fast-food restaurant. What did you eat? Besides the food, name three good things about your experience.

2. Why do some people dislike fast-food restaurants? Do you agree with their complaints?

3. Why do you think there are so many fast-food restaurants?

Read

This online magazine article discusses the many reasons behind the worldwide expansion of fast-food restaurants.

The Fast-Food Revolution

Maurice and Richard McDonald made a lot of money with their restaurant, but they grew tired of the stresses of ownership. The brothers were tired of searching for

5 replacements when their cooks and waitresses quit. They were tired of replacing broken dishes and glassware and lost silverware. Before **abandoning** their successful business, however, they decided to try a new system of preparing and serving food.

A NEW KIND OF RESTAURANT

10 Their remodeled restaurant **contrasted** with the original. It served just hamburgers, cheeseburgers, french fries, and drinks. Paper wrappers and paper cups replaced the dishes and glassware. Silverware wasn't needed because the restaurant didn't serve any food that required a knife, fork, or spoon to eat. The professional cooks were gone, too. Instead, food

15 preparation was divided among several workers, each with a specific task. One worker fried the hamburgers; another wrapped them in paper; a third cooked french fries; and another poured drinks. There were no servers. Customers ordered food and paid for it at a counter. Then they carried their own food to a table. This new system was like a factory assembly line.

20 Increasing the speed of food preparation increased the kitchen's **output** and lowered its costs. The system revolutionized the restaurant business and introduced the term "fast food."

ANOTHER FAST-FOOD RESTAURANT IS BORN

Carl Karcher heard that a nearby restaurant was
25 selling cheap, **albeit** top-**grade** hamburgers for 15 cents. He was charging 35 cents for burgers in his own restaurant. When he visited the McDonald's restaurant, he was astonished to see dozens of customers waiting in line to buy 15-cent
30 burgers while the assembly-line kitchen staff efficiently prepared their food. He **acknowledged**

An early McDonald's restaurant

that this new restaurant system was a good business model. In 1956, Karcher opened his own fast-food restaurant and named it Carl's Jr.

Around this time, Ray Kroc, a salesman who sold milkshake machines to
35 restaurants, also visited the new McDonald's restaurant. Kroc was impressed by its food preparation system. He persuaded the McDonald brothers to sell him the authority to build more McDonald's restaurants across the United States. By 1960, Kroc had opened 250 of them. A **decade** later, there were nearly 3,000 restaurants in the McDonald's restaurant chain, all owned by one corporation.

THE GROWTH OF A NEW INDUSTRY

40 The fast food industry grew because it was born at the right time. One factor was that the U.S. **economy** was **expanding**. The young people in the 1950s were an optimistic **generation**. They were **inclined** to believe that they would be successful in life if they worked hard.

Another important factor that led to the enormous growth of the fast food
45 industry was the automobile. New technology had made automobiles dependable, affordable and easy to drive. People bought new automobiles and wanted to go places. A national highway system, **expanded** during the 1950s, enabled U.S. families to drive long distances. They needed gasoline stations where they could refuel their vehicles and
50 restaurants where they could eat. In time, hundreds of new gasoline stations were built along the highways. These were **complemented** by new fast-food restaurants where travelers could eat a quick meal.

THE MODEL SPREADS

The McDonald's food service model was widely copied in
55 these new restaurants, often by inexperienced owners who wanted to get rich quickly. Some of the new restaurants failed, but many succeeded. Like McDonald's, some even **expanded** into nationwide chains with hundreds of restaurants throughout the country. Among the

A popular fast-food chain in Japan

60 **contemporary** start-ups in the 1950s and 1960s were Burger King, Wendy's, Domino's Pizza, and Kentucky Fried Chicken (KFC).

These restaurants and others that copied the McDonald's system revolutionized the food-service business. The successful chains of restaurants that were created soon inspired other kinds of retail businesses to form their 65 own national chains. Clothing stores, movie theaters, car rental agencies, bookstores, shipping services and hotels are just a few of the businesses that established nationwide chains. By the 1970s, the chain store business model was rapidly spreading overseas to other countries, where domestic companies created their own nationwide business chains.

70 Although many people worldwide **rejected** the idea of globalization, business chains were soon **overlapping** their national borders. National chains became international chains. By 2010, overseas businesses had become common in many countries around the world. A model for fast-food restaurant service helped to revolutionize business throughout the world.

Reading Comprehension

Mark each sentence as *T* (True) or *F* (False) according to the information in Reading 1. Use your dictionary to help you understand new words.

___ 1. Maurice and Richard McDonald abandoned their restaurant because the output was low and it did not make enough money.

___ 2. Their original restaurant used glassware for drinks. In contrast, the new restaurant used paper cups.

___ 3. McDonald's hamburgers were top-grade but very expensive.

___ 4. In the decade between 1960 and 1970, McDonald's expanded to around 3,000 restaurants nationwide.

___ 5. Among the contemporary start-ups of the 1950s and 1960s were Domino's Pizza and Wendy's.

___ 6. In the 1950s, people were optimistic, albeit inclined to worry about the economy.

___ 7. This generation rejected fast foods because they acknowledged the new food preparation system was not efficient.

___ 8. Many roadside stops included the complement of a gas station and a fast-food restaurant.

___ 9. Many business chains are overlapping U.S. borders into other countries.

READING SKILL   Reading Numerical Tables

LEARN

Numerical tables can provide a lot of information in a small space. The information is usually arranged in rows and columns, which makes it easy to read and to compare facts. To preview a table or chart:

1. Read the title to see what kind of information is given.
2. Read the labels at the top of each column.
3. Note the date of the table so that you will know how recent the information is.

APPLY

Read the table. Then, use the information to answer the questions below.

2011 Fast-Food Franchises			
Restaurant	**Start-Up Year**	**Franchises Worldwide**	**Countries With Franchises**
KFC	1952	11,000	60
Pizza Hut	1958	10,000	90
Burger King	1954	12,200	73
McDonald's	1955	31,000	122

With a partner, find answers to these questions in the chart.
1. What year did Burger King start up?
2. How many countries have a Pizza Hut restaurant?
3. Which restaurant has the most franchises worldwide?
4. Which restaurant started most recently?

Vocabulary Activities   STEP I: Word Level

A. With a partner, use the target vocabulary in the box to complete this story. Use the words in parentheses to help you.

abandon	albeit	generations	inclined
acknowledges	expand	in contrast	rejecting

The people of past _____ ate in restaurants only on weekends or
(1. *people born at about the same time*)

special occasions. _____, people today are _____ to
(2. *showing a difference*)   (3. *likely*)

eat out several times a week. This could be a problem if their menu choice is always

a hamburger and french fries. Nearly everyone _____ that too much
(4. *agrees that it's true*)

fat in the diet is not healthy. Unfortunately, hamburgers and french fries are high in

fat, _____ delicious. Instead of _____ fast food
(5. *although*)   (6. *refusing*)

altogether, people should simply _____ the burgers and fries and
(7. *stop having*)

_____ their food choices by ordering something different.
(8. *increase*)

B. Write the length of each time period. Consult your dictionary, if needed.

1. a week   _7_ days   4. a millennium   ___ years

2. a decade   ___ years   5. a millennium   ___ decades

3. a century   ___ decades   6. leap year   ___ days

C. *Output* refers to the production of something or the amount of something produced. With a partner, match the output on the right with the person, machine, or business that produces it on the left. Then take turns creating sentences.

*The **output** of an automobile factory is new cars.*

___ 1. an automobile factory   a. stories

___ 2. a movie studio   b. milk

___ 3. a bakery   c. films

___ 4. an author   d. electricity

___ 5. a power plant   e. cakes and pies

___ 6. a dairy   f. new cars

A *generation* is the group of people (in a family or a society) who are approximately the same age.

> *Americans born in the late 1960s and 1970s are informally called "**Generation X.**"*

People who are approximately the same age are *contemporaries* (noun).

> *Your **generation** liked rock and roll. My **contemporaries** prefer hip-hop.*

The adjective *contemporary* is used to refer to things that happen or exist at about the same time.

> *The increase in use of automobiles was **contemporary** with the growth of fast-food restaurants.*

Another common use of the adjective form is to describe styles that are modern or current in areas such as art, music, or literature.

> *The hotel was a beautiful example of **contemporary** architecture.*

CORPUS

D. In a small group, discuss some of the things that make you and your contemporaries different from your parents' generation.

E. With a partner, match each item from the past with a contemporary invention that has the same function. Discuss how each contemporary invention changed the way that people live or work.

___ 1. dial telephone   a. microwave oven

___ 2. wood-burning stove   b. word processor

___ 3. ceiling fan   c. air conditioner

___ 4. typewriter   d. cell phone

The verb *complement* is related to the word "complete." It is used to refer to things that go well together because, together, they make something complete or better. The adjective form is *complementary*.

> *Caramel corn is delicious. The sweet caramel **complements** the salty popcorn.*

In this unit, complement is also used to mean "a set or group."

> *It takes a **complement** of eight workers to run this restaurant.*

Note: Be careful not to confuse *complement* with *compliment*. To compliment someone means "to praise or express admiration for someone."

> *The customer **complimented** the waiter for his excellent service.*

F. Circle the word that correctly completes each sentence. Compare answers with a partner.

1. This picture frame and that painting (*compliment* / *complement*) each other.

2. Maria was grateful for her teacher's (*complimentary* / *complementary*) remarks.

3. The tan shirt (*compliments* / *complements*) the brown suit.

4. Business partners should have (*complimentary* / *complementary*) skills so that one can manage the finances and the other can manage the employees.

Vocabulary Activities | STEP II: Sentence Level

The phrase *in contrast* is used to show the difference between <u>two</u> people, objects, or events.

> *Desserts do not provide vitamins. **In contrast**, fruits and vegetables are vitamin-rich.*

Use the phrase *to contrast with* when showing a difference between two things.

> *The sweet chocolate **contrasted** nicely with the salty pretzel.*

Albeit (pronounced all–BE-it) is more common in written language than in speech. It is used to show a difference within <u>one</u> person, object, or event. *Albeit* is similar to "but" or "although."

> *The French fries were delicious, **albeit** greasy.*

G. In your notebook, write sentences about fast-food restaurants, using each pair of items and the words in parentheses. Compare sentences with a partner.

1. wash glasses / throw away paper cups (*in contrast*)

   *Restaurants wash glasses. **In contrast,** fast-food places throw away paper cups.*

2. the burger was good / the burger was small (*albeit*)

3. broken chairs / shiny new tables (*contrast*)

4. a parent's idea of a good lunch / her child's idea of a good lunch (*contrasting*)

5. soft drinks $1.25 / water free (*in contrast*)

6. the tiny salad / the enormous hamburger (*contrast*)

When you *abandon* something, you leave it because you don't want it or can't use it. Sometimes you give it up just temporarily.

> The house finally collapsed after the owners **abandoned** it many years ago.

> The snow was so deep that drivers had to **abandon** their cars and walk home.

To *abandon* a plan or a task means to stop before you have completed it.

> I had to **abandon** my plans to travel last summer because I got sick.

When you *reject* something, you refuse to accept it. This verb is commonly used to refer to ideas or plans rather than objects. It is also often used to refer to people who are not accepted for jobs. The noun form is *rejection*.

> Centuries ago, people **rejected** the idea that the earth revolved around the sun.

> Brad offered to drive, but we all **rejected** the offer.

> The University **rejected** Ted's application. He got a letter of **rejection** yesterday.

CORPUS

H. Complete these sentences, in your notebook, with your own ideas. Use a form of *abandon* or *reject* in each one. Compare sentences in a small group.

1. In fast-food restaurant parking lots, there are paper cups and wrappers . . .

2. Babies are sensitive to new tastes, so they may . . .

3. Some fast-food restaurants tried selling vegetable burgers, but . . .

4. When the economy is slow, restaurant chains that planned to expand may . . .

5. We planned to go out to dinner, but when it started to rain . . .

6. The manager offered us a free dessert, but we . . .

Before You Read

Read these questions. Discuss your answers in a small group.

1. Do you know someone who owns a small business? If so, what kind of business is it?

2. What would be some good things about owning your own business? What would be some negative things?

3. How many retail business chains can you name? Take turns naming them.

🔊 Read

This excerpt from a business textbook defines what a franchise is and discusses the advantages and disadvantages of owning one.

Franchising

At one time, all small retail businesses, such as clothing stores, restaurants, shoe stores, and grocery stores, were owned by individuals. They often gave the stores their own names:
5 Lucy's Dress Shop, Fred's Coffee Shop, Johnson Family Grocery. For some people, owning a business fulfilled a lifelong dream of independent ownership. For others, it continued a family business that dated back several **generations**.
10 These businesses used to line the streets of cities and small towns everywhere. Today, in **contrast**, the small independent shops in some countries are almost all gone, and chain stores like The Gap, Starbucks, and 7-Eleven have moved in to replace

At one time, all small businesses were owned by individuals or families.

15 them. Most small independent businesses couldn't compete with the giant chains and eventually failed. However, many owners didn't **abandon** retail sales altogether. They became small business owners once again through franchises. The franchise system is a **contemporary** business model that has increasingly dominated the small business sector of retail trade over the last few **decades**.

A FRANCHISE DEFINED

20 A franchise is a legal and commercial agreement between an individual and a parent company. It gives the person permission to own one of the company's franchise outlets, to use the company name, and to sell the products or services of the company. A person must apply for a franchise; however, not all applicants are approved. Some may be **rejected** because of
25 poor financial histories, for example. If approved, the new business owner (the franchisee) must pay a large start-up fee to the company (the franchiser) and agree to follow its regulations. These regulations require complete uniformity in all of its franchises. This means that the franchiser establishes the rules for the appearance of the store, both inside and
30 outside. It means the franchisee can sell only the products or services of the parent company. It means that a "large coffee" must be the same size in every company franchise. It means that all restaurants in a franchise system must put the same number of pickles on their burgers, and use identical napkins, paper cups, and food wrappers. It also means that the franchisee
35 is **graded** regularly on its performance by the parent company.

Not all chain stores are franchises. Some are owned and operated by the parent company. In **contrast,** a franchise is owned by the franchisee. Restaurants are the most common franchises. On any city block you are likely to see at least one franchise restaurant, and often three or four. In
40 some shopping centers, the entire **complement** of stores is made up of franchises. Almost any kind of business can be franchised, including dental offices, hardware stores, hotels, gas stations, pet hospitals, tax consultants, fitness centers, cleaning services, movie theaters, and child care centers.

ADVANTAGES OF OWNING A FRANCHISE

Despite the restrictions, there are many advantages
45 to owning a franchise. The most important advantage is the support and assistance of the franchiser. For example, the franchiser can help a new owner find a good location, help plan an efficient use of floor space, and help decide on the
50 amount of goods needed to start up the business. The franchiser also provides detailed training for the owner and staff in all areas of the business. Once established, the franchisee benefits from ongoing research and development by the company to keep the business up-to-date and competitive. Company
55 consultants and a network of fellow franchisees offer opportunities to discuss business problems. All these support services provide small business owners with the tools of big business, **albeit** not for free.

There are other advantages to owning a franchise. It helps to own a business with the name of a well-known corporation with an **acknowledged**
60 reputation for good service. Customers are **inclined** to shop at stores with familiar names, and more shoppers mean more sales. Also, individual franchises benefit from the **output** of expensive advertisements paid for by the company, which might **overlap** with local advertising by franchisees. When this happens, there is an extra benefit. Finally, the franchisees are not
65 employees of the company. They are business owners, motivated to work hard to make their businesses successful.

DISADVANTAGES OF OWNING A FRANCHISE

The major disadvantage of the franchise model is the close **economic** relationship among the many franchisees and the parent company. For instance, if one franchisee in the
70 system is found guilty of cheating customers, it reflects poorly on the other franchisees in the system. As a result, all the stores may lose customers. Similarly, if the company makes poor business decisions, the entire chain of franchises may be affected. Finally, the business owners
75 must share their profits with the parent company to pay for the many support services that the company provides.

SPREAD OF THE FRANCHISE MODEL
The success of the franchise system has led to a great **expansion** in the number of small businesses all over the world. Tried first in the United States, the franchise

80 model has spread rapidly to other countries. It has revolutionized retail business in many places, improved the **economic** status of individuals, and strengthened local **economies.** ■

Reading Comprehension

Mark each sentence as *T* (True) or *F* (False) according to the information in Reading 2. Use your dictionary to check the meaning of new words.

___ 1. Franchising is a contemporary business model that has dominated the small business sector for a few decades.

___ 2. A franchisee's business is rarely graded by the parent company.

___ 3. In some shopping centers, the entire complement of stores is made up of fast-food restaurants.

___ 4. Companies provide services to their franchise owners, albeit not for free.

___ 5. There is a business advantage to owning a franchise with the name of a company with an acknowledged reputation for good service.

___ 6. Customers are inclined to shop at stores with familiar names.

READING SKILL Reading Numerical Tables

APPLY

Preview this table. Write the answers to the questions below in your notebook. Compare answers with a partner.

2011 Start-Up Costs for Selected Franchises	
Franchise	**Start-Up Cost** [1]
Burger King	1,200,000–2,800,000
Hampton Inn (hotels)	3,716,000–15,148,800
Dunkin' Donuts	537,750–1,765,300
Subway (sandwiches)	84,300–258,000
Kumon Math & Reading Centers	33,000–130,000
McDonald's	996,000–1,842,700
Midas (auto repair)	380,000–528,000

[1] in U.S. dollars

1. The start-up cost for each franchise is given as a range from the minimum cost to the maximum cost. Using the minimum costs, rank the franchises from the lowest to the highest start-up cost.

2. Using the maximum costs, rank the franchises from the lowest to the highest start-up cost.

3. Which franchise has the smallest range between its minimum and its maximum start-up costs? Which has the greatest range? Can you guess why there is a range in the start-up costs for each company?

4. Amounts in the millions, such as $2,800,000, might be listed on a chart as $2.8 million. We say this number as: "two point eight million dollars." With a partner, read aloud all of the start-up costs greater than one million dollars.

REVIEW A SKILL **Identifying Examples** (See pp. 52–53)

With a partner, identify the many examples related to franchising that are included in Reading 2 (such as the kinds of businesses that can be franchised).

Vocabulary Activities STEP I: Word Level

A. To *grade* something is to rate it or rank it by some quality. With a partner, imagine that you work for a large fast-food corporation. Your assignment is to create grading standards that inspectors can use to grade individual franchise restaurants. Which of these would you include in your grading standards?

___ The kitchen is clean.   ___ The french fries are crispy.

___ The owner wears glasses.   ___ There is soap in the restrooms.

___ The food was ready quickly.   ___ The workers live nearby.

___ The workers wear clean uniforms.   ___ The cashier is friendly.

Think of two more standards to add. What kind of grading standard would you have for your list? Consider these possibilities:

Yes/No   A, B, C, D, F   Pass/Fail   Excellent/Good/Poor

B. Use the target vocabulary in the box to complete this story. Use the words in parentheses to help you.

complement	generation	in contrast
contemporary	grade	output
expanded	had an inclination	specific

In 1916, a revolutionary new concept in retail sales was introduced in the United States. The first self-service grocery store, named Piggly Wiggly, opened. Shoppers of this _____ were used to bringing a shopping list to a neighborhood

(1. shared time in history)
store and waiting while a clerk collected their groceries and measured out products like flour and rice from big barrels. _____ , Piggly Wiggly customers

(2. but)
were given baskets and invited to serve themselves. They filled their baskets with packaged flour and rice, canned goods, and other grocery items from the shelves. Store sales increased enormously because customers _____ to buy

(3. were likely)
more when they made their own selections. Soon Piggly Wiggly _____

(4. increased in size)
into a chain of stores, and other markets copied the self-service model. The
_____ supermarket was born, influencing not only the way people

(5. the modern)
shopped, but also other aspects of the food business. For example, food suppliers

increased their profit because their _____ increased. In order to
(6. production)
attract customers, they used more attractive packaging to _____ the
(7. go together with)
better _____ of food they began to use. They also lowered their
(8. quality)
prices, and began advertising their brand-named products.

To *acknowledge* something means to admit or agree that it is real or true.
The noun form is *acknowledgment*.

> Sam **acknowledges** that the supermarket has lower prices, but he
> still prefers the small market near his house.

CORPUS

C. With a partner, match the beginnings of the sentences on the left with the
endings on the right to make complete sentences. Take turns saying the
complete sentence.

___ 1. I acknowledge that English is difficult,   a. but I don't want one.

___ 2. I acknowledge that air travel is fast,   b. but I hate to cook.

___ 3. I acknowledge that exercise is good for you,   c. but I'm very lazy.

___ 4. I acknowledge that cats are good pets,   d. but I hate to fly.

___ 5. I acknowledge that it's cheaper to eat at home,   e. but I'm a fast learner.

When two things *overlap*, part of one thing covers part of the other. The verb
overlap can refer to time, topic, or the position of objects in space. When two
events *overlap*, the second one starts before the first one ends. When two
topics *overlap with* each other, they cover part of the same subject matter.
The noun form is also *overlap*.

> These two meetings **overlap**, so we need to reschedule one of them.
>
> There was a lot of **overlap** between the lecture on computers and the one on
> Internet technology.
>
> A fish's scales **overlap** each other to protect the skin beneath.

CORPUS

D. Look at this schedule of history classes on Monday at State College. Then
discuss with a partner which classes overlap in time and which overlap in
subject matter. What changes do you suggest?

Class	Time
Roman History	8:00–9:30
Europe from 1850 to Present Day	9:00–10:30
The History of the Middle East	10:30–12:00
Roman and Greek History	1:30–3:00
Europe from 1800 to 1900	3:00–4:00
The History of China	3:30–5:00

To *expand* means "to grow or increase." The noun form is *expansion*. The adjective form is *expansive*. It means "covering a wide area."

> The **expansion** of the library took nearly a year to complete.

> People are happy with the **expansive** new parking lot at the store.

E. Restate these sentences in your notebook, using the form of *expand* in parentheses.

1. The McDonald's menu now includes salads. (*has expanded*)

2. By 2011, the network of McDonald's franchises covered 119 overseas countries. (*expansive*)

3. Recently, McDonald's growth has been faster overseas than in the United States. (*has been expanding*)

4. Many McDonald's franchises have added a children's play yard to increase their appeal to families. (*expand*)

Word Form Chart			
Noun	**Verb**	**Adjective**	**Adverb**
economy economics economist	economize	economic economical economy	economically

The noun *economy* refers to the operation of a country's money supply, industry, and trade. The term *the economy* is often used to refer to the financial situation of a particular nation. The adjective form related to this meaning is *economic*.

> In a healthy **economy,** almost everyone who is able to work has a job.

> **The economy** may be weakened by recent labor strikes.

> Franchising has benefited the **economies** of many developing countries.

> **Economic** growth has slowed in recent months.

Another common use of *economy* (noun) is to refer to the careful use of time, money, and materials. The verb form related to this meaning is *economize*. The adjective form is *economical*.

> Fast-food kitchens are examples of **economy**: no food is wasted, no time is wasted.

> A restaurant might try to **economize** by serving smaller portions.

> It may not be **economical** for a store to stay open extra hours per day.

Economy is also an adjective form that is used to describe products.

> Buy the giant **economy** size. You'll save money.

Economics is the science that studies systems of production, distribution, and use of goods and services. An *economist* is an expert in economics.

> Professor Brown teaches **economics**. He is an **economist** as well as a business owner.

F. Complete the paragraph, using forms of *economy*. Then compare your work with a partner.

Giant retail stores make a small profit on each item they sell, but they depend on making a large number of sales. Their goods are (1) _____ priced to attract customers. Shoppers are pleased that they can (2) _____ by buying products in large, (3) _____ sizes. They believe that it is (4) _____ to buy more and pay a lower price. (5) _____ have studied the effect of a giant store on the local (6) _____ of cities where they are located. They believe that the (7) _____ impact is great. Many small stores are forced to close because they cannot compete with the giant retailers.

If someone *is inclined to* do/be something, it means he or she is likely to do/ be it, based on his or her nature, personality, or experience. The noun form, *inclination*, can also be used to express the same meaning, as in the phrase *to have an inclination* (to do something).

> Steve **is inclined to** be very careful with his money.
>
> He **has an inclination** to look for bargains whenever he goes shopping.
>
> She'll probably learn the piano easily because she's very musically **inclined**.

Note: *Incline* (noun, pronounced IN-cline) refers to a slope.

> When parking on an **incline**, be sure to set your car's brake.

CORPUS

G. In your notebook, write sentences that include these ideas. Use a form of *incline* in each.

1. people who are very hungry / eat too much

   *People who are very hungry are **inclined** to eat too much.*

2. a teenager's eating habits / toward fast food

3. people who can't swim / (not) own sailboats

4. babies / cry a lot

5. little sisters / copy their big sisters

H. Self-Assessment Review: Go back to page 97 and reassess your knowledge of the target vocabulary. How has your understanding of the words changed? What words do you feel most comfortable with now?

Writing and Discussion Topics

With a partner or a small group, share ideas about the following topics. Then have each person write a paragraph about one of the topics.

1. What are some changes that a fast-food restaurant might have to make when it opens a franchise in another country? Consider, for example, the food, the people, and the local customs.

2. Why are small, independent retail businesses inclined to disappear when franchise stores open nearby?

3. Many companies are now creating franchises in developing countries. Do you think these franchises help or hurt the economies of these countries? Explain your opinion.

UNIT 8

The Autism Puzzle

In this unit, you will

> read about a puzzling brain disorder.
> review finding main ideas in a text.
> increase your understanding of the target academic words for this unit.

READING SKILL Making Inferences

Self-Assessment

Think about how well you know each target word, and check (✓) the appropriate column. I have…

TARGET WORDS	never seen the word before	seen the word but am not sure what it means	seen the word and understand what it means	used the word, but am not sure if correctly	used the word confidently in *either* speaking or writing	used the word confidently in *both* speaking and writing
AWL						
🔑 **appropriate**						
assess						
🔑 **capable**						
constrain						
infer						
interact						
🔑 **link**						
mature						
🔑 **odd**						
🔑 **participate**						
🔑 **phase**						
predominant						
ratio						
🔑 **relax**						
🔑 **task**						

🔑 Oxford 3000™ keywords

 Outside the Reading What do you know about autism?
Watch the video on the student website to find out more.

113

Before You Read

Read these questions. Discuss your answers in a small group.

1. Have you ever known a person who had a disability? What was something that he or she was not able to do?

2. In what ways are people with disabilities just like everyone else?

3. What do you know about autism?

MORE WORDS YOU'LL NEED

disability: a condition in your body that makes you unable to use a part of your body properly

◉ Read

This article from a medical website blends information about autism with the story of one autistic child. Notice how the two stories are distinguished from each other.

THE AUTISM PUZZLE

Autism is a little-understood brain disorder. It is marked by poor social and communication skills and by repetitive behavior. Meet two-year-old Shawn, who was just diagnosed with autism.

5 *Shawn sits spinning the wheels of a toy car—spinning, spinning, spinning.*

Shawn's parents have learned that spinning is not a typical **phase** of childhood. It is a common repetitive behavior of autistic children.

10 *"Let's pretend we're cats," Shawn's three-year-old cousin suggests. "Meow," she says, walking on hands and knees. Shawn, also three now, flaps his hands in front of his face.*

Most autistic kids can't pretend because they're not **capable** of imagining something that is not real. The **odd** hand-
15 flapping behavior is common in kids with autism.

*"Let's go to the market," Shawn's mom says. Shawn, now four, hurries to the door and stands waiting. The market is noisy with recorded music and the clatter of shopping carts. Shawn covers his ears and is soon screaming. His mom **infers** that the*
20 *noise hurts his ears.*

Extreme sensitivity to loud or harsh sounds is common in autism. So is sensitivity to bright lights and various textures.

Six-year-old Shawn is watching a Sesame Street videotape. "A B C," it sings. Shawn rewinds the tape and it repeats, "A B C."
25 *His mother calls, "Shawn! Don't rewind the tape." He knows this isn't allowed, but he likes to see the same part over and over. "No rewind," he answers.*

Like most autistic children, Shawn likes repetition, and he can't **constrain** his behavior. His language skills are poorly developed,
30 and he doesn't speak in full sentences.

Shawn's school textbook asks this question: Which of these smells good? (a) a window (b) a flower (c) a lamp. Shawn lifts the book to his nose and sniffs. None of them smells at all, so he leaves the answer blank.

35 Schools usually fail to accurately **assess** the abilities of autistic children because classroom **tasks** are not **appropriate** for them. For instance, many autistic children are not able to **link** a printed word with something that is not real.

Shawn's family goes to visit Grandma and Grandpa. Shawn, now
40 *eight, rings the doorbell, opens the door, and walks in. "Hi, Shawn," says Grandma. He ignores her and turns on the TV. "Did you get wet in the rain?" Grandpa asks. "Yes. Rain," Shawn answers.*

Like most autistic children, Shawn doesn't understand how
45 to behave **appropriately** in social situations, and prefers to be alone. He answers questions that people ask, but doesn't understand the give-and-take of conversation.

Eleven-year-old Shawn is playing baseball. When it's his turn at bat, he hits the ball into the outfield. "Run!" yells the
50 *team coach. Shawn walks toward first base. Meanwhile, Brad picks up the ball and brings it to Shawn. Like all players on this special team, Shawn and Brad have autism.*

Most **participants** on this team are boys. That's because kids with autism are **predominantly** male, with boys
55 outnumbering girls by a **ratio** of 4 to 1. Autistic kids may have excellent physical skills, but they rarely **participate** in team sports because they don't understand the rules.

Shawn is doing math homework. He writes fast, and in less than five minutes he has solved 25 multiplication problems.

60 Some autistic children do well at school subjects, but most do not. Shawn is very bright, but not academically **mature**. His

speaking and listening skills are poor, but in school he is good at math and spelling. He enjoys looking at photographs, and he likes maps and calendars. He
65 frequently writes letters to Grandma and Grandpa describing places his family has visited.

It's bedtime. Shawn showers and puts on pajamas. He brushes his teeth and climbs into bed. "I love you," says Mom, giving him a kiss. "I love you," Shawn repeats and
70 *closes his eyes.*

Shawn is asleep. Finally, his handsome face and sturdy body **relax**.

Reading Comprehension

Mark each sentence as *T* (True) or *F* (False) according to the information in Reading 1. Use your dictionary to check the meaning of new words.

___ 1. Shawn's parents at first thought that spinning was a typical phase of childhood.

___ 2. Autistic kids are not capable of imagining something that is not real.

___ 3. It is difficult for autistic kids to constrain their odd behavior.

___ 4. Shawn's mother inferred that he liked the loud music in the market.

___ 5. Autism seems to be linked to the sex of a child.

___ 6. Autistic girls outnumber autistic boys by a ratio of 4 to 1.

___ 7. Autistic kids seldom participate in team sports because they don't interact with other kids.

___ 8. Schools are usually unable to assess the abilities of autistic children because classroom tasks are not appropriate for them.

___ 9. Autistic kids may be bright, but they are not academically mature.

___10. Autistic kids are predominantly male, so most of them have excellent physical skills.

___11. Autistic children can relax when they are sleeping.

LEARN

To *infer* is to use indirect information or evidence to come to a decision or a logical conclusion. Parents of an autistic child must often use *inference* to understand their child's behavior because the child may not be able to explain what he wants or what he doesn't like. For example, in Reading 1, there is a sentence:

> In the market, Shawn covers his ears and is soon screaming. His mom **infers** that the noise hurts his ears.

Shawn's mother *made an inference* based on what she saw. Maybe she was correct, or maybe she wasn't, but it was a logical conclusion.

Read these excerpts from Reading 1. What can you infer from the information? More than one answer may be possible.

APPLY

1. "Let's go to the market," Shawn's mom says. Shawn hurries to the door and stands waiting.
   - ✓ a. Shawn understands his mother's words.
   - ✓ b. Shawn obeys his mother.
   - ___ c. Shawn is in a good mood today.

2. Shawn rewinds the videotape and it repeats, "A B C."
   - ___ a. Shawn knows how to operate a tape player.
   - ___ b. Shawn likes to sing along with the tape.
   - ___ c. Shawn likes the ABC song.

3. "Which of these smells good?" Shawn lifts the book to his nose and sniffs. None of them smells at all.
   - ___ a. Shawn has a poor sense of smell.
   - ___ b. Shawn can read.
   - ___ c. Shawn expected the words to smell.

4. "Did you get wet in the rain?" Grandpa asks. "Yes. Rain," Shawn answers.
   - ___ a. Shawn likes the rain.
   - ___ b. Shawn likes Grandpa.
   - ___ c. Shawn understands Grandpa's question.

5. "Let's pretend we're cats," Shawn's three-year-old cousin suggests.
   - ___ a. Shawn's three-year-old cousin can talk.
   - ___ b. Shawn's three-year-old cousin can pretend.
   - ___ c. Shawn's three-year-old cousin has a cat.

REVIEW A SKILL Finding the Main Idea (See p. 21)

Each story about Shawn (except the last one) is followed by a paragraph that describes a typical behavior of autistic children. Make a list of the main ideas of each paragraph in your notebook.

A. Read this magazine article that gives advice to parents of autistic children. Use the target vocabulary in the box to complete the article. Compare results with a partner.

appropriate	capabilities	interact	participate	relax
assess	constrain	mature	phases	task

Experts recommend that parents enroll young children with autism in a special preschool class as early as possible. The goal is to help the children strengthen their social and language skills during the formative _____ of childhood
(1. time periods)
and learn _____ classroom behavior before they enter kindergarten.
(2. proper)
Each day, the children _____ in games, songs, and play activities that
(3. take part)
encourage them to _____ with each other. Individual children are
(4. mix together)
assigned a daily _____, such as feeding the class pet, to help teach
(5. small job)
responsibility. Parents are required to attend classes with their child to learn more about autistic behavior. Observing their own child in a group setting allows them to realistically _____ the child's _____ and limitations.
(6. judge) (7. strengths)
Parents also see techniques that the trained teachers use to _____ a
(8. limit)
child's unwanted behavior, such as hand-flapping. Telling a child to
_____ by taking a deep breath is one technique parents learn. As the
(9. become less tense)
children _____, they will remember this relaxation technique and
(10. grow up)
use it to constrain their own behavior without being reminded.

B. A *link* is a connection between two things. Certain behaviors are linked to autism because they are common or typical in most autistic people. Working with a partner, put a check (✓) next to the behaviors that are linked to autism, according to Reading 1.

___ a. spinning   ___ d. being sensitive to loud noises   ___ g. excelling at math

___ b. writing letters   ___ e. watching a videotape   ___ h. hand-flapping

___ c. pretending   ___ f. preferring to be alone   ___ i. liking repetition

C. A *phase* is a step or stage of development. With a partner, look at the phases of language development in children. Number them in the order they are likely to occur, with the first phase as *1*.

___ a. one-word sentences ("Ball.")   ___ d. two-word sentences ("Mama look.")

___ b. babbling ("Dadadada")   ___ e. three-word sentences ("Daddy, read me.")

___ c. cooing ("Oooooooo")   ___ f. crying

The adjective *odd* refers to something that is unusual or inappropriate for a particular situation.

> Some autistic kids have the **odd** behavior of hand-flapping.

Another meaning for *odd* applies to numbers. An odd number cannot be divided evenly by 2, such as the numbers 1, 3, 5, 7, 9, 11, 13, etc.

> I always seem to have an **odd** number of socks in my drawer.

As a plural noun, *odds* refer to the chances of something happening.

> The **odds** are one in a million that you will win the lottery.
>
> I wouldn't give you good **odds** on finding a taxi at this hour of night.

CORPUS

D. Check (✓) the combinations that you think make odd drinks. Discuss your choices with a partner.

___ coffee with sugar   ___ coffee with mustard   ___ milk with honey

___ tea with honey   ___ coffee with milk   ___ milk with cola

___ tea with garlic   ___ tea with lemon   ___ hot chocolate with chili pepper

Vocabulary Activities   STEP II: Sentence Level

Word Form Chart			
Noun	**Verb**	**Adjective**	**Adverb**
assessment reassessment	assess reassess	assessable	_____

E. To *assess* something is to judge it or to form an opinion about it. Complete this paragraph about autism assessment by using a form of *assess* in each blank.

By age two, a typical child has developed many verbal and social skills, such as speaking and interacting with others. If these skills are absent, the child's doctor may suspect autism. There is not just a single test a doctor can use to (1) _____ a child for autism. Instead, the doctor looks for the presence or absence of certain behaviors. Autism is (2) _____ only by carefully observing the behavior of a child, so the actual (3) _____ may take several hours. The doctor (4) _____ the child's attempts to communicate with his parents. He also looks for repetitive behavior, such as hand-flapping, or sensitivity to sounds or textures. If the doctor's diagnosis is autism, he may suggest a (5) _____ by a second doctor to confirm the diagnosis. Over the next several years the child will be (6) _____ regularly to see if he has made progress.

F. A *task* is a small job, often one that is assigned by a teacher, parent, or boss. Using what you know of Shawn's skills from Reading 1, infer which of these classroom tasks will probably be difficult for him and which he will do easily. Write sentences in your notebook about each task.

1. writing about his vacation

   Shawn can probably do this **task**. *He often writes letters to his grandparents about places he visited with his family.*

2. taking a spelling test

3. solving subtraction problems

4. working with a committee to plan a class party

5. giving an oral report

The adjective *appropriate* refers to something that is suitable, proper, or correct for a particular situation. People sometimes disagree about what is appropriate or inappropriate. The noun form is *appropriateness*.

   What is **appropriate** *to wear to a job interview?*

   Meg is **appropriately** *dressed in a suit. Jeans and a T-shirt are* **inappropriate**.

   The interviewer commented on the **inappropriateness** *of Sam's clothes.*

As a verb, *appropriate* means "to decide to give something, especially money, for a particular purpose." The noun form is *appropriation*. This meaning is rather formal and official.

   The university **appropriated** *one million dollars for a new autism study.*

   The business plan includes an **appropriation** *for local charities.*

CORPUS

G. Read these short conversations. Some of Sam's responses are odd. Write a sentence about the appropriateness of Sam's reply using the word in parentheses.

1. Mark: "Thank you for the birthday card."

   Sam: "How old are you?"

   (*appropriate*) _____

2. Mark: "Are you coming to my party tonight?"

   Sam: "Thank you."

   (*appropriate*) _____

3. Mark: "Can I borrow your pen?"

   Sam: "I know how to spell."

   (*inappropriate*) _____

4. Mark: "Have you seen my brother?"

   Sam: "No."

   (*appropriate*) _____

Before You Read

Read these questions. Discuss your answers in a small group.

1. Think of some common illnesses. What causes them?

2. Think of some common illnesses. How are they cured?

3. Why might a pharmaceutical company be willing to fund research into the causes of autism?

Read

This journal article details some of the current research into autism and some possible causes for it.

Looking for Answers

Autism is a neurological disorder that usually appears before a child's third birthday. It is marked by impaired language skills, impaired social skills, and repetitive behaviors.

RECENT INCREASE IN AUTISM

Recently there has been a dramatic and unexplained increase in the
5 number of children diagnosed with autism. Medical scientists estimate an autism **ratio** of 1 in every 110 children in the United States. Other countries show similar high **ratios**: 1 in 160 in Australia, 1 in 250 in India, and 1 in 475 in Japan, for example. Scientists believe that
10 the differences among countries may reflect how children are evaluated rather than the actual proportion of children who have autism. These numbers are alarming to scientists because they do not know what causes autism and do not know how
15 to cure it. Medical researchers have been looking for answers.

Temple Grandin holds a doctorate degree. She also has autism.

THE AUTISM SPECTRUM

Scientists use the term "autism spectrum" to refer to the range of abilities that autistic people display. At one end of the spectrum, individuals are severely
20 affected, while at the other end, individuals are only mildly affected. Some individuals cannot speak; others are highly verbal. Some are overly sensitive to noise; others seem not to notice it. Some prefer to be alone; others want friends. Some even marry and have children. Some are unable to learn school subjects; others go on to earn a Ph.D. degree.
25 Indeed, each person with autism may have a unique set of traits.

LOOKING FOR CAUSES OF AUTISM

Although scientists agree on the traits that characterize autism, they have not yet found what causes autism. In the 1950s, autism was considered a psychological disorder, caused by "refrigerator mothers." Their personalities were thought to be so cold and uncaring that their children grew up unable
30 to speak or **interact** with others. As research progressed, scientists realized that autism was actually a neurological, or brain, disorder. Studies have identified several areas of the brain that differ from the norm in autistic individuals. These areas involve emotions, critical thinking, learning, and paying attention. However, no one area seems to hold the key to autism.
35 Some researchers have **inferred** that faulty connections between areas of the brain may be responsible for autism. Or perhaps there are too many connections. That could cause an overload of messages within the brain.

Medical scientists have also explored brain chemistry. In a recent study, researchers took blood samples from many
40 newborns. When some of these babies later developed autism, the researchers tested their early blood samples and found high levels of four chemicals that influence the early **phases** of brain development. However,
45 they have not been able to prove a direct **link** between the chemicals and the autism.

There is strong agreement that genes, the carriers of inherited traits, play a role in autism. Research continues to explore
50 heredity as a cause. Recently, researchers found a **link** between autism and the age of the child's father, with the **odds** of parenting an autistic child increasing with older fathers. It is also known that among autistic children, males **predominate** by
55 a **ratio** of 4 to 1. Additionally, autism seems to run in families. Despite the strong evidence pointing to heredity, scientists haven't yet identified a single gene responsible for autism. Instead, they now think that hundreds of changes take place in a child's genes before birth. Some of these changes affect connections between brain cells. When genetic changes involve
60 connections in the brain, autism can occur.

Scientists are also investigating environmental causes. They have looked into toxic metals in water and soil, harmful chemicals in household products, viruses, air pollution, and even television viewing, but have not found a consistent **link** to autism. Recently, some scientists have suggested that a
65 combination of hereditary and environmental factors may cause autism.

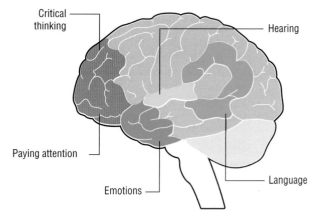

Areas of the brain commonly affected by autism

TREATING AUTISM

Despite this extensive research, scientists so far have been unsuccessful in finding either a cause or a cure for autism. However, treatment, either through medication or training, has benefited many autistic children by helping them to **relax**, to **constrain** antisocial behavior, to **participate**
70 socially, and to learn useful skills. Medication has worked for some children. However, it has not been widely used because it can have serious side effects. Other treatments that have worked for some children include

controlling the child's diet, providing the child with an animal to
take care of, and encouraging self-expression through art. The
75 Chinese use acupuncture and **relaxation** programs.

APPLIED BEHAVIOR ANALYSIS

A common training is Applied Behavior Analysis, which breaks
down a **task** into tiny steps and rewards every small success with a
bit of cookie or other treat. If a child does not speak, for example,
the therapist will reward even a small sound a child makes when
80 she asks him to repeat a word. It may take several sessions to get
the child to utter a sound, and many more to get him to say a word,
but each success is praised and rewarded. Many autistic children
have improved greatly with such training, but others have not.
    Whatever treatment parents decide is **appropriate,** they must be
85 aware that children are most likely to benefit if they begin early.
Delaying treatment until the child **matures** is a waste of valuable
time. Parents must also recognize that not all treatments benefit
every child, so they must regularly **assess** their child's behavior for signs
of progress. Treatment that doesn't work is also a waste of time.
90   Meanwhile, scientists are still looking for answers to solve the autism
puzzle. ■

Scientists have yet to solve
the "autism puzzle."

Reading Comprehension

Mark each statement as *T* (True) or *F* (False) according to the information in
Reading 2. Use your dictionary to check the meaning of new words.

___ 1. Researchers found four chemicals that influence the early phases of brain
development.

___ 2. As a man gets older, the odds increase that he will parent an autistic child.

___ 3. There is strong agreement that heredity is the predominant cause of autism.

___ 4. Researchers have found a link between autism and television viewing.

___ 5. Medication has helped some autistic children constrain their behavior.

___ 6. Children who participate in Applied Behavior Analysis learn a task one step
at a time.

___ 7. Parents must regularly assess their child's behavior for signs that they are
wasting time.

APPLY

Reread the paragraphs indicated. Then, write *D* for the ideas that are directly stated and *I* for those that you can infer. Write *N* if an idea is not directly stated or cannot be inferred. Discuss your answers in a small group.

PARAGRAPH 2

_D_ 1. Scientists do not know the cause of autism.

___ 2. There is no cure for autism.

_I_ 3. Scientists cannot explain the recent increase in autism.

___ 4. Scientists are not sure how many children are affected.

___ 5. Scientists are alarmed.

PARAGRAPH 3

___ 1. A person who is mildly affected with autism is highly verbal.

___ 2. Some people with autism are very intelligent.

___ 3. Not all autistic people prefer to be alone.

___ 4. The term "autism spectrum" was recently created.

___ 5. Each autistic person may have a different combination of traits.

PARAGRAPH 4

___ 1. Autism is not a psychological disorder.

___ 2. A neurological disorder is a disorder involving the brain.

___ 3. Scientists are not certain if faulty connections within the brain cause autism.

___ 4. Scientists have abandoned their study of the brain.

___ 5. Several areas in the brain of autistic children differ from those in normal kids.

Vocabulary Activities   STEP I: Word Level

A person who is *capable* of doing something has the necessary skills to do it. If he lacks these skills, then he is *incapable* of doing it. The words can also refer to objects.

> Most autistic children are **incapable** of imagining something that is not real.

> Passenger airplanes are **capable** of flying overseas without refueling.

CORPUS

A. With a partner, decide which of these activities a blind person is capable or incapable of doing. Take turns making sentences with this information.

*A blind person is **capable** of listening to music.*

✓ listening to music   ___ riding on a bus   ___ telling jokes

___ driving a car   ___ reading a newspaper   ___ using a telephone

To *relax* means to stop working and rest. It can also mean to make your body less tense by loosening your muscles.

*When he sleeps, Shawn can finally **relax** and get some rest.*

To *relax* <u>something</u> means to make it looser or more flexible.

*Teachers often **relax** <u>classroom</u> <u>rules</u> for students with disabilities.*

CORPUS

B. Complete each sentence with *relax* or *relax it*.

1. I've worked hard all day. It's time to ___*relax*___ .

2. Sometimes you can cure a headache if you just _____ .

3. The law against speeding is too strict. I wish the government would

   _____ .

4. Don't pull the rope so tight. Can you please _____ ?

5. I often play the piano to _____ .

Word Form Chart			
Noun	**Verb**	**Adjective**	**Adverb**
constrain constraints	constrain	constrained unconstrained	_____

C. To *constrain* someone or something is to hold them back or limit their actions. With a partner, decide which behaviors you think parents should constrain in their children.

___ 1. studying   ___ 4. playing   ___ 7. laughing

___ 2. screaming   ___ 5. watching TV   ___ 8. arguing

___ 3. sleeping   ___ 6. fighting   ___ 9. surfing the Internet

D. The plural noun *constraints* is a more formal way of describing limits. Match the formal language with its more informal version.

___ 1. I have financial constraints.

___ 2. I have medical constraints.

___ 3. I have time constraints.

___ 4. I have transportation constraints.

___ 5. I have family constraints.

___ 6. There are legal constraints to selling my house.

a. I promised my parents I would visit them.

b. I have to finish this by tomorrow.

c. My car won't start.

d. I can't afford that right now.

e. I need to see a lawyer about this.

f. I'm not healthy enough to do that.

Word Form Chart			
Noun	**Verb**	**Adjective**	**Adverb**
maturation maturity immaturity	mature	mature immature maturational	_____

To *mature* refers to the process of becoming fully developed physically or mentally. If someone or something is *immature*, then development is delayed compared to others.

>As boys **mature**, they become taller and more muscular.

>Susan is ten, but she's so **immature**.

There are two noun forms:

maturation   the process of developing or aging
maturity   the state of being fully developed

 CORPUS

E. Read this paragraph. Then, complete it by using the correct form of *mature* from the chart. Compare answers with a partner.

A premature baby is one that is born before it is fully developed. Because of its

(1) _____, a premature baby is usually placed in a hospital incubator

where it can continue to (2) _____ in a safe environment. A baby born

too soon has not had time for adequate (3) _____ of body systems

that are essential for life. The baby's (4) _____ lungs, for example, may

not be able to supply enough oxygen, so it will need help breathing. The baby will

remain in the incubator until it has achieved a safe level of (5) _____.

The baby will make steady progress, but its growth will be delayed compared to

that of a full-term baby. For example, a full-term baby may sit up at six months of

age, but a premature infant may not reach this (6) _____ phase for

several more months.

Word Form Chart			
Noun	**Verb**	**Adjective**	**Adverb**
predominance	predominate*	predominant	predominantly

*Note: There is no *–ing* form for this verb.

Predominance and its related word forms refer to being greater in importance, strength, number, or some other factor.

> Tall players **predominate** in the game of basketball. They are **predominant**.
>
> There is a **predominance** of brown-eyed people in the world.
>
> Humans are **predominantly** brown-eyed.

CORPUS

F. Read the paragraph about Temple Grandin. Then, rewrite the sentences that follow in your notebook, using the form of *predominant* in parentheses.

Temple Grandin is autistic, yet she has a Ph.D. and is a university professor. Dr. Grandin has written several books about autism. Her superior verbal skills and intelligence have enabled her to analyze and describe how individuals with autism think. She writes, "I think in pictures. Words are like a second language to me. I translate both spoken and written words into full-color movies."

1. Among high-functioning autistic individuals, most are visual thinkers. (*predominance*)

   *There is a **predominance** of visual thinkers among high-functioning autistic people.*

2. Nouns are easiest because they are mostly things you can picture. (*predominantly*)

3. Most people are verbal thinkers in universities. (*predominate*)

4. Dr. Grandin was surprised by the number of people who think only in words. (*predominance*)

5. Seeing pictures in her mind is the way Temple Grandin creates ideas. (*predominant*)

G. A *ratio* is a mathematical expression comparing the size or amount of two sets of things. Write a sentence in your notebook to express the ratios of these groups. Discuss your sentences in a small group.

1. at birth: boys, 105; girls, 100

   *At birth, boys outnumber girls by a **ratio** of 105 to 100.*

2. autistic children: girls, 1; boys, 4

3. adults who are colorblind: men, 15; women, 1

4. at age 65: women, 10; men, 7

5. people in my family: male, _____; female, _____

6. communication I receive: email, _____; phone calls _____

7. school time: hours in class, _____; hours studying, _____

Word Form Chart			
Noun	**Verb**	**Adjective**	**Adverb**
participant participation	participate	participatory	_____

H. Read this description of an autism study. Then, complete the paragraph by using the correct form of *participate* in each blank. Compare answers with a partner.

Several young children are asked to (1) _____ in an experiment. Half of the (2) _____ are typical children, and half of the (3) _____ are autistic children. Their (4) _____ consists of watching a scene in which two little girls are playing with dolls. One of the girls, Mary, puts her doll in a basket and leaves the room. While she is gone, her friend, Linda, takes the doll out of the basket and puts it into the drawer of a table. Then Mary returns. The children who are (5) _____ in the experiment are asked, "Where will Mary look for her doll?" The typical children agree that Mary will look in the basket because that's where she left the doll. However, the autistic children say that Mary will look in the drawer because that's where the doll is. This experiment demonstrates that autistic kids cannot imagine something that is not true.

I. Imagine that you were one of the scientists who conducted the above experiment. In your notebook, write a brief conclusion that describes what you learned from the experiment about children with autism.

J. Self-Assessment Review: Go back to page 113 and reassess your knowledge of the target vocabulary. How has your understanding of the words changed? What words do you feel most comfortable with now?

Writing and Discussion Topics

With a partner or a small group, share ideas about the following topics. Then have each person write a paragraph about one of the topics.

1. Why might it be difficult to be friends with an autistic person? What would be some of the challenges?

2. The first reading is called "The Autism Puzzle." Why is this a good title?

3. What are some facts you learned about autism?

UNIT 9

Sea of Life

In this unit, you will

> learn about humans' impact on oceans and important deep-sea discoveries.
> review identifying definitions.
> increase your understanding of the target academic words for this unit.

READING SKILL Reading Statistical Tables

Self-Assessment

Think about how well you know each target word, and check (✓) the appropriate column. I have…

TARGET WORDS	never seen the word before	seen the word but am not sure what it means	seen the word and understand what it means	used the word, but am not sure if correctly	used the word confidently in *either* speaking *or* writing	used the word confidently in *both* speaking *and* writing
AWL						
aggregate						
🔑 annual						
compatible						
🔑 conduct						
🔑 contribute						
erode						
finite						
🔑 impact						
🔑 occupy						
🔑 process						
🔑 temporary						
terminate						
🔑 trace						
🔑 ultimate						

🔑 Oxford 3000™ keywords

 Outside the Reading What do you know about oceanography? Watch the video on the student website to find out more.

Before You Read

Read these questions. Discuss your answers in a small group.

1. How often do you eat fish?
2. Do you ever visit the ocean to go fishing or to relax on a beach?
3. How do oceans benefit people?

🔊 Read

This article is part of a series of articles about our changing oceans.

SAVING THE OCEANS

The oceans of the world **occupy** over 70% of the earth's surface. They provide food for billions of people, serve as places of recreation, and facilitate the transportation of passengers and cargo.

5 For all of human history, people regarded the oceans as an indestructible and **infinite** resource. Until recently, humans had little **impact** on the oceans. However, as the earth's population increases, human activity will

10 **ultimately** destroy the oceans unless immediate steps are taken.

OVERFISHING

Overfishing is one major threat. Fish are being taken out of the oceans faster than the remaining fish can reproduce. A big fish—tuna, cod, shark,

15 or swordfish—yields many pounds of delicious seafood when it reaches maturity. However, to meet the increasing demand for these fish, commercial fishermen began catching small, immature fish. In the **process**, they almost

20 destroyed the species. Ocean scientists estimate that 90% of these big fish are now gone from the oceans, and about 30% of all fished species have been destroyed.

A commercial fishing operation

OCEANS AS A SOURCE OF FOOD

Of the earth's seven billion people, over one billion rely on fish as
a source of protein. Billions more eat fish frequently because of
its health benefits and its good taste. Throughout the world, food
from the sea provides between 5% and 10% of the total food
supply. But when fish disappear from the oceans, they will also
disappear from our dinner plates. The **impact** on those who rely
on fish could be malnutrition or even starvation.

HOW HUMANS IMPACT OCEANS

Humans are **impacting** ocean life not
only by what they take out of the
oceans, but also by what they put into
the oceans. Carelessly discarded cans,
bottles, plastic cups, and baby diapers
find their way into the stomachs of
fish, often killing them. Toxic chemicals
and industrial trash are also discarded
into the oceans, either accidentally or
thoughtlessly. Such **conduct** pollutes
the water and kills sea life. Spills from
a single oil tanker can **contribute**
200,000 tons of oil to the already
polluted oceans. In the United States,
an estimated 15,000 tons of automobile oil **annually** washes off
roads into rivers and streams and **ultimately** into the sea.

Trash that has ended up in
the ocean

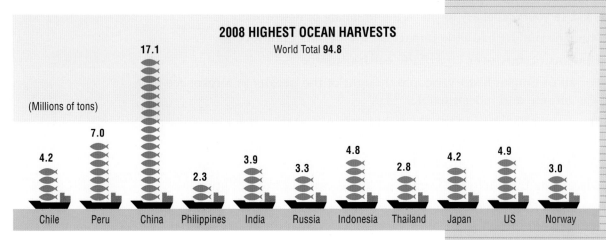

2008 HIGHEST OCEAN HARVESTS
World Total **94.8**

(Millions of tons)

Chile	Peru	China	Philippines	India	Russia	Indonesia	Thailand	Japan	US	Norway
4.2	7.0	17.1	2.3	3.9	3.3	4.8	2.8	4.2	4.9	3.0

Along with the harmful oil, however, run-off also carries tons of
nutrients in the form of plant matter, fertilizers, animal waste,
and garbage that can be **traced** to cities, farms, factories, and
forests. Poisonous algae and bacteria (microscopic plants and
animals) in the ocean feed on the nutrients. As the run-off
increases, the **aggregation** of algae and bacteria increases,
further **eroding** the marine environment. Small fish that feed on the
algae and bacteria are sickened or killed by the poisons they
contain. When larger fish feed on the smaller ones, they too are

sickened by the poisons. **Ultimately,** humans who eat the flesh of poisoned fish will be sickened, too.

STEPS THAT CAN SAVE THE OCEANS

Are healthy oceans **compatible** with an industrialized world? What can be done to **terminate** the steady destruction of the
60 oceans? Among other steps, countries can set limits on the number of fish that fishermen can legally catch. Governments can also create sea reserves, areas where fishing is **temporarily** banned until the fish population increases. Commercial enterprises can develop open-ocean aquaculture to grow fish in
65 underwater cages miles from land. And individuals can refuse to buy fish in restaurants and markets if the species is threatened.

Governments can also protect the sea by enacting strict controls on ocean dumping. They can demand that oil tankers have higher safety standards. They can **process** run-off water to remove toxic
70 substances. Individuals can properly dispose of leftover household and garden chemicals so they do not add to the toxic run-off into the oceans.

Scientists agree that it's not too late to save the oceans, but we must begin at once to take the necessary steps.

Reading Comprehension

Mark each sentence as *T* (True) or *F* (False) according to the information in Reading 1. Use your dictionary to check the meaning of new words.

___ 1. Human conduct had little impact on the oceans until recently.

___ 2. Humans occupy over 70% of the earth's surface.

___ 3. For all of human history, people thought of the oceans as a resource that was infinite and indestructible.

___ 4. Steps must be taken to terminate human activity that may ultimately erode the quality of the oceans.

___ 5. Overfishing may temporarily benefit certain species of fish.

___ 6. Discarding trash into the oceans greatly contributes to pollution.

___ 7. Increases in the aggregation of algae and bacteria can be traced to the nutrients in run-off from cities, farms, factories, and forests.

___ 8. Oil tankers annually spill 200,000 tons of oil into the oceans.

___ 9. It isn't possible to process run-off water to remove toxic substances.

___10. Healthy oceans are compatible with an industrialized world if necessary steps are taken to protect the oceans.

LEARN

Articles about scientific topics frequently contain statistics that support the information in the text. The table in Reading 1, for example, compares the amount of fish collected, or harvested, by several nations of the world to support the information about overfishing.

Numerical information in tables is often reduced for clarity. The table in Reading 1 eliminates the many zeros in the numbers by telling the reader that amounts are in million tons. So, for Chile, the number 4.2 really means that Chile harvested 4,200,000 tons of fish. Shortened numbers are read differently from complete numbers. Chile's harvest is read "four point two million tons."

Numbers in tables are also often rounded up or down. The actual number of fish might be 4,198,314 tons, for example, but that number is rounded up to 4.2 million tons.

APPLY

A. Complete the tasks with a partner. Use the information in the table in Reading 1.

1. In the order of their fish harvests, read all of the country names and their fish harvests out loud. Use shortened numbers, such as "Chile—four point two million tons."

2. From biggest harvest to smallest, write all of the complete numbers, such as 4,200,000. Then, read them out loud.

B. What can you infer from the information in the table? Mark a statement *I* if you can infer that it is true. Mark a statement *N* if you cannot infer that it is true.

_N_ a. The United States harvested more fish in 2008 than in 2007.

___ b. Fishing is an important industry in these countries.

___ c. About half of the top countries are in Asia.

___ d. Indonesia harvested more fish than Norway.

___ e. The numbers do not include fish caught in rivers and lakes.

___ f. All the fish is eaten by people within the country that harvests it.

___ g. China harvested about 18% of the world total in 2008.

___ h. Canada did not harvest fish in 2008.

REVIEW A SKILL Identifying Definitions (See p. 69)

Find definitions in Reading 1 for the words *nutrients* and *algae*.

A. Use the target vocabulary in this unit to complete these analogies. Then write the type of relationship each analogy has: example, synonym, antonym, action, or part. (See Unit 1, page 13, for more on analogies.)

Relationship

1. start : end AS begin : _____   _____

2. house : permanent AS tent : _____   _____

3. grow : build AS destroy : _____   _____

4. player : team AS part : _____   _____

5. phase : development AS step : _____   _____

B. *Erosion* is the gradual process of something being destroyed or worn away. It can describe natural or biological processes or more abstract ideas. The verb form is *erode*. With a partner, decide what might cause the erosion of the following.

1. mountains   4. a store's reputation

2. a person's health   5. a person's plans to travel

3. the soil on a farm   6. a friendship

The verb *aggregate* (pronounced AG-gre-gate, with a slight stress on the last syllable) means to collect items into one body or mass.

> *The company will* **aggregate** *its small stores into one superstore.*

The adjective form is spelled the same way but is pronounced slightly differently (AG-gre-git, no stress on the last syllable).

> *The* **aggregate** *effect of pollution is depletion of sea life.*

The noun has two forms: *aggregate* (pronounced like the adjective) and *aggregation*.

CORPUS

C. With a partner, decide what to call an aggregation of these items. More than one answer is possible.

1. an aggregation of stores: _____ *a shopping mall, a shopping center* _____

2. an aggregation of books: _____

3. an aggregation of plants: _____

4. an aggregation of people: _____

5. an aggregation of printed pages: _____

D. An annual event is one that occurs once a year or is repeated every year. With a partner, check (✓) the events that occur annually. When in the year do they take place?

___ spring   ___ your birthday   ___ new classes

___ New Year's Day   ___ a wedding   ___ animal migration

___ a full moon   ___ October   ___ family gatherings

When something is *finite* (pronounced FI-nite, rhyming with SKY-light), it is fixed in space or amount and can be measured.

*The amount of oil in the world is **finite**. When we use it up, there is no more.*

Something *infinite* (pronounced IN-fi-nit) is without limits. This word is often used for something that seems endless, very great, or not measurable.

*She is **infinitely** patient with the children in her class.*

E. With a partner, match each sentence on the left with one on the right that has the same meaning.

___ 1. The oceans seem infinite.   a. There sure are lots of them.

___ 2. Oil tankers hold a finite amount of oil. b. They seem to go on and on.

___ 3. Whales have a finite number of teeth.   c. They're really interesting.

___ 4. There's an infinite number of fish species. d. They don't grow new ones.

___ 5. I am infinitely fascinated by whales.   e. They can't hold any more.

F. With a partner, use the target vocabulary to complete this article on the impact of global climate change.

annual	contributed	impact	traced
compatible	erosion	process	ultimately

Today there are 20,000 to 25,000 polar bears worldwide. This represents a decline of 21% over the last 20 years that can be directly (1) _____ to global climate change. As the average (2) _____ ocean temperature in the Arctic rises, the bear population declines. The bears' way of life is not (3) _____ with a warm climate because they depend on sea ice for summer hunting. The (4) _____ of global climate change has caused an (5) _____ of the polar bear environment. It has (6) _____ to weight loss in the males, falling reproduction rates in the females, and lower survival rates among newborn cubs. If the overall warming (7) _____ of global climate change continues at its present rate, the polar bears will (8) _____ disappear.

Vocabulary Activities STEP II: Sentence Level

When people or things are *compatible*, they get along well or work together well. The negative form is *incompatible*. The noun forms are *compatibility* and *incompatibility*.

*Ahmed and Hakim were successful business partners because they were **compatible**.*

*Electrical appliances are often **incompatible** with foreign power systems.*

G. Work with a partner. Imagine that one of you has an old computer. That person goes to a computer store to buy some new equipment and software for it. The other person is a clerk in a computer store. Create a short conversation that includes the words *compatible, incompatible, compatibility,* and *incompatibility* in at least two questions and two answers between the two people.

A: *Is this printer* **compatible** *with my computer?*

B: *Actually,* **incompatibility** *is often a problem with these older models.*

The word *impact* has two meanings. It can refer to a strong force hitting something, or more abstractly, to the strong effect something has or creates. Both meanings have a noun and verb form.

We felt the **impact** of the explosion a mile away.
The world economy **impacts** all our lives.

CORPUS

H. In your notebook, rewrite each sentence two ways, using *impact* once as a noun and once as a verb.

1. The shortage of fish has affected the fishing industry.

    The shortage of fish has had an **impact** *on the fishing industry.*
    The shortage of fish has **impacted** *the fishing industry.*

2. Her new job affected the whole family.

3. The collision had a different effect on each of us.

4. The new law will change the way people pay their taxes.

To *contribute to* something means to add or give something to a larger activity.

The adjective form is *a contributing + factor/cause/element/etc.*

High winds **contributed** to the accident.
High winds were a **contributing** factor to the accident.

To *contribute* means to give money or assistance, usually to a charity. The noun form is *contribution*.

I **contribute** annually to Save Our Oceans.
I send a **contribution** to the Red Cross, too.

Collocations (words that go together): *to make/send a contribution*

CORPUS

I. In your notebook, rewrite the following sentences to include a form of *contribute*.

In April 2010, an explosion of an oil rig caused a massive oil spill in the Gulf of Mexico. BP owned the rig.

1. BP admitted to mistakes that helped cause the oil spill.

    BP admitted to mistakes that **contributed** *to the oil spill.*

2. Oil rose to the surface of the ocean. Strong winds made the oil spread over 4,000 square miles.

3. BP gave $20 billion to build a fund to help pay for damages and clean-up.

4. Thousands of volunteers gave money and time to help rescue sea animals.

Before You Read

Read these questions. Discuss your answers in a small group.

1. Some people claim that we know more about the moon than we know about our oceans. Do you agree?

2. What is the value of exploring the ocean floors?

3. Who should pay for exploring the oceans? Why?

Metric conversions for measurements used in Reading 2:
1 inch = 2.54 centimeters   1 pound = 0.45 kilogram
1 foot = 0.3 meter   1 knot = 1.85 km/hour
1 mile = 1.6 kilometers

Read

This article about underwater exploration appeared in a science magazine.

Exploring the Deep Ocean

Alvin can dive to ocean depths of 20,000 feet—nearly four miles down. Alvin can rest on the ocean bottom or hover at middle depths for up to ten hours, taking photographs and performing
5 underwater experiments. Alvin is amazing. Many of the 150 to 200 dives Alvin makes **annually** result in underwater discoveries of unusual sights never before seen.

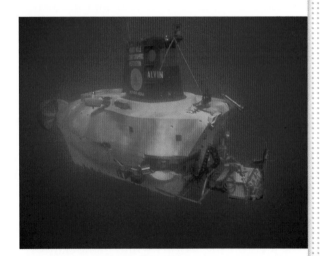

The deep-sea submersible, Alvin

FACTS ABOUT ALVIN
Alvin is not a man. Alvin is a deep-sea
10 submersible craft capable of carrying up to three **occupants**. It is owned and operated by the Woods Hole Oceanographic Institution on the east coast of the United States. Alvin was built in 1964, but it has been upgraded and
15 reconstructed many times since then. Alvin's titanium hull, or outside shell, is built to withstand the **impact** of the immense pressure of the deep ocean. Alvin weighs 37,400 pounds and is 23 feet 4 inches long. It has a six-mile range and a top cruising speed of two knots. Five hydraulic thrusters propel the craft, and lead-acid batteries power the
20 electrical system.

Inside is an **infinite** variety of the latest electronic equipment, including a gyrocompass, a magnometer, and a computer **terminal**.

Alvin allows researchers to **conduct** underwater
biological, chemical, and geological studies. Special lamps
25 shine light into the black water so observers can see the
wonders of the underwater environment. Cameras are
mounted on the outside to take underwater photographs,
and two external "arms" enable researchers to collect
underwater samples.

ALVIN'S AMAZING DISCOVERY

30   One day in 1977, Alvin **contributed** to an amazing
discovery. On that day, Alvin was transporting scientists
on a routine study. The craft was one and a half miles
below the surface of the sea near the coast of the
Galapagos Islands. As they looked through the three
35 12-inch portholes, the scientists were **temporarily**
stunned to see a strange underwater landscape littered
with what looked like chimneys. The chimneys were
discharging clouds of black smoke into the surrounding
water. Clustered around the chimneys was an
40 **aggregation** of odd creatures that lived totally cut off
from the world of sunlight. The scientists were looking at
hydrothermal vents and the strange sea creatures that
exist near them—an entire system of life based not on
sunlight, but on energy from the earth itself.

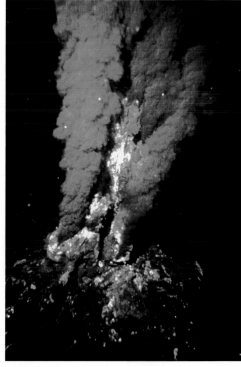

A hydrothermal vent, or "chimney"

STRANGE SEA CREATURES

45 An unusual kind of animal life exists around these
vents. Among the chemicals pouring out of the vents is
hydrogen sulfide, a gas that is poisonous to most land-
based life. However, bacteria in the seawater near the
vents feed on this gas and other dissolved chemicals and
50 minerals pouring from the vents. Then tiny animals feed
on the bacteria, and these tiny animals **ultimately**
become food for still larger animals. Giant red and
white tube worms eight feet tall cluster near the vents
and dominate the scene. Tiny shrimps and white crabs
55 feed on the worms while giant clams rest in the sand. In
an environment that seems **incompatible** with life,
these creatures are thriving.

Ocean life growing near the vents

WHAT IS IN THE FUTURE?

Since the first vent was discovered in 1977, hundreds of other vents have
been located in oceans around the world. In 2008, a cluster of five vents
60 was discovered in the Atlantic Ocean between Greenland and Norway.
Some of the sites are inaccessible, so scientists have not been able to
study them all. However, scientists are planning to **trace** the development
of vents by revisiting some they studied earlier. They want to find out if
the vents will **erode** or remain active over time and if the odd creatures
65 will change. ■

Reading Comprehension

Mark each statement as *T* (True) or *F* (False) according to the information in Reading 2. Use your dictionary to check the meaning of new words.

___ 1. Alvin makes between 150–200 dives annually.

___ 2. Alvin is a man who temporarily helped researchers conduct underwater studies aboard a submersible craft.

___ 3. Alvin's occupants have an infinite variety of electronic equipment available.

___ 4. Alvin contributed to the discovery of the Galapagos Islands in 1977.

___ 5. Near vents, aggregations of giant tube worms, shrimps, and crabs exist in an environment that seems incompatible with life.

___ 6. Scientists plan to revisit some of the vents in order to trace their development.

___ 7. Scientists will terminate their study of vents because some vents are inaccessible.

READING SKILL | Reading Statistical Tables

LEARN

Facts about numbers are often difficult to read when they are included as part of the text of an article. For this reason, scientists and technicians usually create a specification sheet, or "spec sheet," to isolate these numbers.

APPLY

Using information from Reading 2, complete this spec sheet about Alvin. You may use the system of measurement in the article or convert those numbers to the metric system.

Alvin General Specifications	
Length	
Weight	
Maximum Depth	
Maximum Speed	
Range	
Occupants	
Propulsion	
Electrical System	
Equipment (Internal)	
Equipment (External)	

Vocabulary Activities STEP I: Word Level

Something *temporary* exists or is used for only a short time. *Temporarily* is the adverb form.

> The **temporary** ban on tuna fishing ended last week.
>
> Shipping was **temporarily** halted by a tsunami.

CORPUS

A. With a partner, decide which of these are temporary.

___ a summer job	___ a mountain	___ a substitute teacher
___ a street name	___ a rainstorm	___ an oil spill
___ a cloud	___ a full moon	___ an emergency
___ a highway	___ a puddle of mud	___ an ocean

Literally, *ultimate* refers to the last or final thing. More commonly, it is used to indicate an extreme, such as the best or worst. *Ultimately* can mean "finally" or "basically."

> For me, the **ultimate** vacation is two weeks aboard a luxury cruise ship.
>
> We tried to fix it several different ways but **ultimately** decided to buy a new one.

CORPUS

B. With a partner, think of different ways to end these sentences.

1. I waited for a long time, hoping to catch a fish. Ultimately, . . .

   Ultimately, I gave up and went home.

   Ultimately, I caught a big one.

2. We couldn't decide where to eat dinner. My friend wanted Chinese food and I wanted seafood. Ultimately, . . .

3. The turtle struggled to get back into the water. Ultimately, . . .

4. My cell phone was making odd noises. I shook it and banged it on the table. Ultimately, . . .

5. The ultimate in awful food is . . .

6. We are almost finished painting the house. The ultimate step is . . .

Word Form Chart			
Noun	**Verb**	**Adjective**	**Adverb**
terminal termination	terminate	terminal	terminally

The word *terminate* and its forms have many uses, all related to "end" or "ending."

> I **terminated** the agreement with my cell phone company because their service was bad.
>
> Failure to follow the rules will result in **termination** of the game.
>
> Ed was **terminated** after working for the company ten years.
>
> My grandfather has **terminal** cancer.
>
> Her plane arrives at **Terminal** C, Gate 7, at 7:36 p.m.
>
> Each office had forty or more computer **terminals**.

Note: *terminate* cannot be used in place of *ultimate*.

CORPUS

C. With a partner, match each sentence on the left with the one that explains it on the right.

___ 1. Pedro terminated the lease on his apartment.   a. He was fired.

___ 2. Filipe's uncle has a terminal illness.   b. He hung up.

___ 3. Hiro was terminated from his job.   c. He wanted to take a bus.

___ 4. Hans waited at the downtown terminal.   d. He is very ill.

___ 5. Pham spent hours at his desk terminal.   e. He's moving soon.

___ 6. Suhart terminated the phone conversation.   f. He used his computer.

A *trace* is evidence that something happened or existed.

> I could see **traces** of mice in the garage.

A *trace* is also a small bit of something.

> The river had **trace** amounts of toxic substances in it.

To *trace* something is to follow its history or development. Not everything is *traceable*. Sometimes records are lost or unknown.

> The book **traced** the history of deep-sea exploration.
>
> The oil spill was **traceable** to a small tanker in the North Sea.

Another meaning for *trace* is to copy the outlines of a diagram or picture.

> He put a piece of paper over the picture and carefully **traced** its shape.

CORPUS

D. With a partner, match the person on the left with the kind of tracing he or she might do. Take turns making sentences.

_a_ 1. an artist   a. a picture

An artist might **trace** *a picture.*

___ 2. the post office   b. a family history

___ 3. a scientist   c. the life cycle of a whale

___ 4. a grandmother   d. a lost package

___ 5. the police   e. the letters of the alphabet

___ 6. a small child   f. the owner of an abandoned car

Vocabulary Activities STEP II: Sentence Level

The word *conduct* has different meanings in its noun and verb forms.

As a verb, *conduct* (pronounced con-DUCT) refers to something that you organize and carry out. It can also mean to lead an activity or group. This meaning has no other word forms.

> Scientists **conducted** several underwater experiments.
>
> She has **conducted** a number of choirs.

Collocations (words that go together):

an experiment	an investigation	a test	a meeting
an orchestra	a class	a tour	a search
a survey	a demonstration	a project	a discussion

The noun (pronounced CON-duct) is a more formal word for *behavior*.

> This is clearly a case of improper professional **conduct**.

CORPUS

E. Match the people in the first column with an activity in the second column and the purpose or topic of their activity in the third column. Write complete sentences in your notebook using different forms of the verb *conduct*.

*A visiting professor **conducted** a class on the future of sea exploration.*

1. ~~a visiting professor~~	a survey	playing his Symphony in F
2. detectives	~~a class~~	for the missing murder weapon
3. marketers	an experiment	to identify future customers
4. a famous composer	a search	~~the future of sea exploration~~
5. ocean scientists	a local orchestra	on poisonous algae

Word Form Chart			
Noun	**Verb**	**Adjective**	**Adverb**
occupancy occupant	occupy	occupied occupying	_____
occupation	_____	occupational	occupationally

The word *occupy* has several meanings.

To have possession of a particular physical space:

*Do you know who **occupies** that apartment?*

*Hotel rates are based on double **occupancy**; there is an extra charge for a third person.*

To fill a space, a period of time, or one's thoughts:

*Studying **occupied** my weekends until I graduated.*

Politically, to take over a country or area by force and run it:

*A foreign army once **occupied** this country. The **occupation** began in 1850.*

The noun form *occupation* refers to the work that a person does.

*Everyone in my family has the same **occupation**—we're all farmers.*

*A police officer has to face many **occupational** hazards.*

If something is *occupied*, it is in use. If a person is *occupied*, then she is busy.

*The bathroom was **occupied**, so I waited my turn.*

*I am **occupied** all day with meetings.*

C CORPUS

F. In your notebook, rewrite the following sentences to include the given form of *occupy*.

1. There is a computer inside Alvin. (*occupies*)

   *A computer **occupies** space inside Alvin.*

2. Dr. Lee works as an ocean scientist. (*occupation*)

3. Alvin has room for three people. (*occupants*)

4. Scientists spend most of their time looking out of the view ports. (*occupies*)

5. Giant tube worms live in an underwater environment without sunlight. (*occupy*)

Process refers to change. A *process* can refer to a natural event that occurs in gradual steps or a series of actions directed toward a particular result.

> The **process** of tree growth can be traced through its rings.

> How did an author ever write a book without a word **processor**?

> From the **processing** plant, the **processed** fish is transported to markets.

Process can also refer to checking information, fees, or other materials submitted in order to achieve something.

> The university **processes** thousands of applications for admission.

The phrase *in the process* can suggest two different ideas. In one context, it means a person has started a complex procedure but has not completed it yet.

> Helen is **in the process** of finishing her essay for her college application.

In other contexts, it describes how one action results in something unexpected.

> I was cooking dinner, and **in the process** I burned my thumb.

 CORPUS

G. In your notebook, rewrite each sentence to include the form of *process* in parentheses. Be prepared to read your sentences aloud and discuss them in a small group.

1. Scientists observed how vents are formed. (*the process of*)

   *Scientists observed the **process** of vent formation.*

2. Vents are formed when seawater seeps down into the earth's crust. (*the process of . . . begins*)

3. The seawater is heated to over 750° F. As it heats, it expands. (*in the process*)

4. As it rises through the cracks, the hot water dissolves chemicals from the rock. (*in the process of*)

5. Some of the minerals harden and form a rim around the vent. (*in the process*)

H. Self-Assessment Review: Go back to page 129 and reassess your knowledge of the target vocabulary. How has your understanding of the words changed? What words do you feel most comfortable with now?

Writing and Discussion Topics

With a partner or a small group, share ideas about the following topics. Then have each person write a paragraph about one of the topics.

1. Describe some of the ways that oceans contribute to the economies of countries around the world.

2. One result of global warming will be that polar ice will melt. What impact will this have on our world?

3. Describe some of the ways that oceans are used for recreation. Could any of these contribute to a depletion of sea life? How?

UNIT 10

Giving Nature a Hand

In this unit, you will

> read about old and new ways to help people overcome disabilities.
> review identifying time and sequence words.
> increase your understanding of the target academic words for this unit.

READING SKILL Distinguishing Fact from Opinion

Self-Assessment

Think about how well you know each target word, and check (✓) the appropriate column. I have...

TARGET WORDS	never seen the word before	seen the word but am not sure what it means	seen the word and understand what it means	used the word, but am not sure if correctly	used the word confidently in *either* speaking *or* writing	used the word confidently in *both* speaking *and* writing
AWL						
advocate						
🔑 alternative						
confine						
discriminate						
🔑 error						
evaluate						
🔑 impose						
incentive						
🔑 objective						
🔑 proportion						
🔑 sum						
suspend						
tense						
voluntary						

🔑 Oxford 3000™ keywords

Before You Read

Read these questions. Discuss your answers in a small group.

1. How many people do you know who wear glasses? What would their lives be like if they didn't own a pair of glasses?

2. What does it mean to "give someone a hand"? How can people give nature a hand to keep their bodies healthy?

3. How has science helped people have healthier bodies?

Read

This article highlights some of the ways that humans have managed to overcome the obstacles that nature put in their way.

Giving Nature a Hand

For most of human history, humans have had to live with the body that nature gave them. They lacked the knowledge to improve eyes that couldn't see clearly, or help ears that couldn't hear.
5 Such disabilities were more than an inconvenience for early humans; they were a threat to their existence. A person with impaired vision might not be able to hunt or work with tools, for example. Over time, the **incentive** to survive led people to develop devices
10 that would fix these impaired conditions.

EARLY WAYS TO IMPROVE VISION

During his 12th-century travels through China, Marco Polo supposedly saw people using eyeglasses. Soon, eyeglasses came into common use in Italy. The **objective** of the earliest lenses was to help people see things that were close up so they could do tasks like carving or sewing. Soon after, lenses to
15 help people see distant objects became common. In the 18th century, the two types of lenses were combined in one pair of bifocal lenses so individuals who were both farsighted and nearsighted needed just one pair of eyeglasses.

Early glasses were held in the hand or clipped on the nose, held there
20 by the **tension** of the stiff wire they were made from. Modern framed glasses, **suspended** from the ears by earpieces, were uncommon until the 19th century.

IMPROVING VISION TODAY

Nowadays, other options are available. For example, about 2 percent of the people in the world opt for contact lenses, which lie on the surface of the
25 eye. Fortunately, corneal implants and laser surgery may one day eliminate the need for corrective devices altogether.

WAYS TO IMPROVE HEARING

No evidence exists of an early device to enhance hearing, but it probably did exist. It was likely a hollow, cone-shaped animal horn with the point cut off. Held with the
30 tip by the ear, the horn could be directed toward a voice, for example, so sound waves from the voice could be focused into the ear.

In the 20th century, battery-operated hearing aids became common. The components included a case that
35 contained a battery and a sound-amplification device. A wire attached the device to a disc that was inserted into the ear. Today, thanks to electronics, tiny devices that fit behind the ear contain both energy cells and an amplifier. They provide not only better amplification, but also better
40 **discrimination** between various sounds. There is now a surgical **alternative** to improve hearing without an external device. A medical **evaluation** can determine whether this **alternative**—a cochlear implant—might be right for someone with a hearing loss.

An early hearing aid

REPLACING TEETH

45 Tooth loss was common among our early ancestors due to accidents, infection, and disease. Being toothless affected people's ability to eat and speak clearly. It also made them physically unattractive. The earliest known false teeth, or dentures, date from the 15th century, when rich people were willing to spend a large **sum** of money for uncomfortable false teeth carved from ivory, animal
50 teeth, or wood. When the process of making rubber was perfected in 1851, dentists immediately **advocated** its use as a base material for dentures. It was soft, so it would be comfortable. It could be molded to fit individual mouths, and it could securely hold artificial teeth. It was also cheap, making dentures affordable to everyone.

55 Today, dental implantation is available for people who need to replace one or several teeth. Fixed into the jawbone with a titanium screw, an implanted tooth becomes a permanent replacement rather than a removable dental device.

The exploration of an ancient Mayan burial site in Honduras
60 uncovered the tomb of a young woman, **confined** there for 1,400 years. Her jawbone contained three tooth-shaped pieces of seashell embedded into the bone in spots where three of her natural teeth were missing. Was the dental implant a punishment **imposed** on her, or was it a **voluntary** procedure? Were the Mayans the first humans to give nature a hand with
65 dental implants? ■

Reading Comprehension

Mark each statement as *T* (True) or *F* (False) according to the information in Reading 1. Use your dictionary to check the meaning of new words.

___ 1. Survival is a strong incentive to fix impairments.

___ 2. The objective of the earliest eyeglasses was to help people do close-up tasks.

___ 3. Early eyeglasses were secured to the ears by tension or suspended from the nose.

___ 4. A large proportion of people are choosing to have corneal implants to eliminate the need for corrective devices.

___ 5. A penalty was imposed on people for using animal horns as hearing aids.

___ 6. A medical evaluation may determine that a person's hearing would improve with a cochlear implant.

___ 7. Better sound discrimination is possible in modern hearing aids.

___ 8. Dentists advocate the use of corneal implants as an alternative to dentures.

READING SKILL   Distinguishing Fact from Opinion

LEARN

As you read, it is important to recognize the difference between a *fact* and an *opinion*.

FACT   information that can be proven to be right or wrong

OPINION   a statement that you cannot prove to be either right or wrong

Opinions often contain value words such as *best, worst, beautiful, awful, funniest,* or *most interesting.* Compare these two statements:

> It is raining.
> The weather is awful.

You can prove the first statement by looking out of the window. The second statement is someone's opinion of the weather, so you cannot prove it is right or wrong.

APPLY

A. With a partner, decide whether each statement is a fact or an opinion. Write *Fact* or *Opinion* on the line.

_____ 1. Humans cannot live without oxygen to breathe.

_____ 2. Good vision is more important than good hearing.

_____ 3. Humans have five toes on each foot.

_____ 4. People with big ears can hear better.

_____ 5. Long eyelashes are pretty.

_____ 6. Type O is the most common blood type.

B. Write one fact and one opinion about devices to improve hearing. Write one fact and one opinion about devices to improve vision. Read your sentences aloud in a small group and let the others decide which are facts and which are opinions. Discuss any statements that you disagree about.

C. Look again at Reading 1. Scan the article to find one sentence that states an opinion. (Hint: It's about dentures.)

REVIEW A SKILL **Identifying Time and Sequence Words** (See p. 84)

Scan Reading 1. What words are used to identify the present time in the development of each type of device?

_____

_____

Vocabulary Activities STEP I: Word Level

The adjective *objective* is related to facts and opinions. A text or observation is considered objective if it only deals with information that is based on facts, not emotions. The opposite is *subjective,* meaning based on personal opinions.

OBJECTIVE   It is raining.

SUBJECTIVE   The weather is awful.

Objectivity is the noun form and *objectively* is the adverb form.

> Readers sometimes question the **objectivity** of a news article.

> Newspapers try to report the news **objectively**, without personal opinion.

The noun *objective* has a different meaning. It is a formal alternative for *goal* or *aim*.

> The inventor's **objective** was to create contact lenses for animals.

CORPUS

A. With a partner, match the medical device on the left with its *objective.* Take turns making sentences describing the connections.

*The **objective** of dentures is to substitute for missing teeth.*

<u> c </u> 1. dentures   a. to improve declining eyesight

___ 2. hearing aids   b. to attain improved hearing

___ 3. eyeglasses   c. to substitute for missing teeth

___ 4. cochlear implants

___ 5. contact lenses

___ 6. dental implants

B. Imagine that these sentences appeared in a newspaper article. With a partner, cross out the subjective words so that the statements become an objective report of the news.

1. At a public meeting yesterday, our ~~popular~~ mayor advocated suspending the ~~ridiculous~~ city tax on sunglasses.

2. The audience applauded wildly after his convincing speech.

3. The administration made a terrible decision that affected many people when it foolishly imposed this tax.

4. Last year the tax generated only the tiny sum of $63.00.

5. After many long and boring comments from angry citizens, the meeting finally ended at 8:00.

C. Read this paragraph about ways of straightening teeth. Use the target vocabulary in the box to complete the sentences. Use the words in parentheses to help you.

advocate	incentive	proportion
impose	confined	tense
alternative	objective	voluntarily

Nowadays, many adults _____ the discomfort of dental braces on
    (1. *force*)

themselves _____ . It will be the second time around for a large
        (2. *willingly*)

_____ of adults who are considering braces. One day they notice
    (3. *part*)

that teeth which were perfectly aligned in childhood have shifted and may even

overlap. Dentists _____ braces for them. Their _____
            (4. *recommend*)   (5. *goal*)

is to prevent future health problems. However, the patients' _____ is
                                                          (6. *motive*)

usually to improve their appearance. Standard braces are made of steel, but a

popular _____ for adults are clear plastic bands. The first few days
          (7. *choice*)

with new braces are the worst. The pain in their mouth makes patients feel

_____ . Often the pain is not _____ to the mouth.
    (8. *stressed*)   (9. *limited*)

Patients may temporarily experience headaches and earaches, too. However, when

the braces are ultimately removed, most adults say that the discomfort was worth it.

Tension refers to how tightly something is stretched. It can describe the
forces acting on objects or the emotional forces acting on people.

  *The dentist increases the **tension** in my braces a little more each week.*

  *Don's been so **tense** since he lost his job. He's been having **tension** headaches.*

  *The atmosphere was **tense** as the doctor removed the bandages from the*

  patient's eyes.

In grammar, *tense* refers to the time of a verb.

  *The past **tense** form of "keep" is "kept."*

CORPUS

D. With a partner, think of things that might make these people feel tense. What is the cause of the tension?

1. someone getting on an airplane
2. the hostess of a large party
3. someone who cannot hear
4. someone going to a job interview
5. a teacher on her first day of school
6. a new parent

E. An *incentive* is something that encourages a person to do something. With a partner, match the incentive with the action that will make it possible. Take turns making sentences with the matches.

_c_ 1. having a nice smile   a. getting dentures

*Having a nice smile is an **incentive** for getting braces.*

___ 2. being able to see clearly   b. exercising every day
___ 3. being able to hear conversations c. getting braces
___ 4. being able to chew food   d. giving up smoking
___ 5. having big muscles   e. wearing a hearing aid
___ 6. improving your health   f. wearing glasses

Vocabulary Activities STEP II: Sentence Level

The word *sum* has several uses, all related to the idea of a total amount of something. In math, for example, the *sum* is the result you get when you add numbers together.

> *The **sum** of 6 + 2 + 3 is 11.*

It is also the total value of a group of things.

> *A team is only as good as the **sum** of its players.*

It can refer to an amount of money.

> *Most insurance pays you a large **sum** when disaster strikes.*

The phrase *sum up* means to state the main points of a text or conversation.

> *The doctor **summed up** the situation in three words: "You need glasses."*

A *summation* is a formal review of the main points of something, written or spoken.

> *The jury listened carefully to the lawyer's three-hour **summation**.*

CORPUS

F. **Look again at Reading 1. Check (✓) the statement that accurately sums up each of these paragraphs.**

PARAGRAPH 2

___ 1. Some people cannot see things at a distance.

___ 2. Certain lenses are for farsighted people.

___ 3. The history of eyeglasses began many centuries ago.

PARAGRAPH 3

___ 1. Modern ways to correct vision are different from earlier ways.

___ 2. About 2 percent of people in the world wear contact lenses.

___ 3. After the 19th century, glasses had earpieces to hold them on.

Now, write statements that sum up these paragraphs. Use *in summation* or *to sum up* in each statement.

1. PARAGRAPH 4: *To sum up, effective hearing devices didn't become available* *until the 20th century.*

2. PARAGRAPH 5: _____

_____

3. PARAGRAPH 6: _____

_____

To *impose* something on a person is to use authority to require them to obey. *Imposition* is the noun form.

> The city will **impose** a fine on residents who park in the streets overnight.

Unfavorable circumstances can *impose* problems on people.

> Poverty **imposes** many hardships on people.

If someone *imposes on* you, they interrupt your routine and expect a favor from you.

> I don't want to **impose** on you, but may I use your computer?

Someone who is *imposing* is impressive in appearance or behavior and seems powerful.

> Standing before the crowd in full uniform, the general was an **imposing** figure.

CORPUS

G. **With a partner, think of limits that might be *imposed on* people in each category. Then choose one category and write in your notebook a short paragraph that describes three limits.**

Poverty	Blindness	Autism
Poverty imposes many limits on people. One is . . .		

The word *discriminate* has several different meanings related to the idea of differentiation—or noticing differences between things.

> The law should not **discriminate** between famous and ordinary people.

> Mrs. Clifford is very **discriminating.** She only serves the best quality foods.

To *discriminate* one thing from another means to be able to see, hear, smell, touch, or feel the difference.

> I can't **discriminate** one perfume from another. They all smell the same to me.

> He has trouble with color **discrimination** and can't tell lime green from olive green.

To *discriminate* <u>against</u> a person or a group of people is to treat them unfairly.

> In past decades, employers often **discriminated against** women.

> Racial **discrimination** is still common in many places.

It is often difficult to tell which meaning of *discriminate* or *discrimination* is being used. Here are some helpful hints.

When *discriminate* or *discrimination* means "to recognize differences,"

- it is nearly always used with *between* or with *from*.

- two or more similar things are mentioned.

When *discriminate* or *discrimination* means "to treat people unfairly,"

- it is nearly always used with *against*.

- a particular person or a group of people is mentioned.

- a particular type of discrimination is named: for example, *age discrimination*.

CORPUS

H. Rewrite these sentences in your notebook to include a form of *discriminate*. Read your sentences in a small group. Did you convey the correct meaning in each of your sentences?

1. Society is unfair to people who are fat.

2. People who are colorblind usually cannot tell red from green.

3. It is against the law for employers to treat someone unfairly because of his race.

4. Immigrants often face unfair treatment in their new countries.

5. Movie actors wear contact lenses because studios won't hire actors who wear glasses.

6. Lemons and limes taste the same to me.

Before You Read

Read these questions. Discuss your answers in a small group.

1. Eyeglasses, hearing aids, and false teeth are common devices that assist people who have physical limitations. What other devices do you know of that help people's bodies function?

2. Have you ever seen people with artificial arms or legs? What could they do?

3. How do you think artificial limbs will change in the future?

Read

The title of this article refers to a 1970s science fiction television series, *The Six Million Dollar Man.*

BIONIC PEOPLE

The Six Million Dollar Man

ome 40 years ago, a bionic man was the hero in a science fiction television series called *The Six Million Dollar Man.* In the series, an astronaut has a terrible accident. His
5 damaged arms and legs are replaced with high-tech artificial ones costing six million dollars. The new arms and legs made him "bionic"—part human and part machine. More recently, a real bionic man has been created, and for a **sum** nearly
10 as great as the original one. Jesse Sullivan can't run 60 miles per hour, but he does have a bionic arm to replace one he lost in an accident. This new arm is not science fiction. It is the world's first thought-controlled artificial arm.

JESSE'S STORY

15 In 2001, Jesse Sullivan was 54 years old and working as a lineman for an electrical power company. Somehow, he made an **error** and contacted with a live wire on the ground that gave him a 7,200-volt shock of electricity. His arms were destroyed.

After recovering from the accident, Jesse got a set of artificial
20 arms. He controlled them by moving his back muscles and pressing tabs with his neck. He learned quickly and did well, so his doctors at the Rehabilitation Institute of Chicago **advocated** using him as a research subject. He would continue to use a conventional artificial

right arm, but his new left arm would be a 12-pound Neuro-
25 Controlled Bionic Arm. Instead of using his body to move it, he
would use his brain.

Jesse underwent surgery to prepare for this. The **objective** was
to isolate the healthy nerves that once controlled movement in
Jesse's left arm. These nerves were reattached to muscles in
30 Jesse's chest. Eventually the re-routed nerves would grow into
the chest muscles. Finally, electrodes were attached to Jesse's
chest and connected to his artificial arm. Now, when Jesse
tenses these chest muscles, it creates a tiny electrical signal.
The signal activates a computer in the left
35 arm that does what Jesse's brain tells it to
do. The movement is as **voluntary** and as
immediate as it would be in a real arm.

The brain not only gives signals to the
missing arm, it receives them as well. When
40 a doctor touches Jesse's chest in various
spots, it feels to Jesse as if the doctor is
touching his thumb, for instance, even
though his hand and arm are missing.
Eventually he will be able to feel what the
45 bionic hand is touching and to **discriminate**
between sensations of heat and cold.

Jesse Sullivan

This bionic arm is **suspended** from a plastic
framework that fits around Jesse's upper body. It has six motors
and consists of parts from around the world. The hand was made
50 in China, the wrist in Germany, and the shoulder in Scotland. The
six motors move the bionic arm's shoulder, elbow, and hand as
a unit. Jesse uses his arm to help him put on socks, shave, eat,
and do other personal and household chores just by thinking
about them.

CLAUDIA'S STORY

55 In 2004, Claudia Mitchell became the second person to use a
thought-controlled artificial arm. That year the 24-year-old woman
lost her left arm in a motorcycle accident. While she was
recovering from her accident, she worried about her future. She
was very brave. She did not want the accident to **impose**
60 restrictions on her or **confine** her to her house. She saw no
alternatives until she read a magazine article about Jesse
Sullivan and his bionic arm. The article gave her the **incentive** to
try to get her own bionic arm. She said to herself, "I've got to
have one of those."

65 Her doctors **evaluated** her and agreed to make her into a bionic
woman. After surgery, Claudia was fitted with a 10-pound

artificial arm that she controls with her
brain. She mastered the use of her new
arm and entered college.

70 Today a **disproportionate** amount of
research into brain-controlled artificial
arms is focused on implanting sensors
in the brain to link the brain to the arm.
Dr. Todd Kuiken, who heads the neural
75 engineering program at the Chicago
Institute, rejects this approach. He says
of the technique used with Jesse and
Claudia, "The exciting thing about this
technique is we are not implanting anything
80 into (the) body."

Claudia Mitchell

Reading Comprehension

Mark each statement as *T* (True) or *F* (False) according to the information in
Reading 2. Use your dictionary to check the meaning of new words.

___ 1. Jesse's doctors made an error and charged him a sum of six million dollars.

___ 2. The objective of Jesse's surgery was to isolate the healthy nerves that once
controlled the left arm and reattach them to chest muscles.

___ 3. When Jesse tenses his chest muscles, he activates a computer.

___ 4. Someday Jesse's hand will be able to discriminate between heat and cold.

___ 5. Claudia worried that her accident might impose restrictions on her life or
confine her to her house.

___ 6. She saw an alternative when she read about Jesse in a magazine article.

___ 7. The article gave Claudia the incentive to meet Jesse Sullivan.

___ 8. A disproportionate amount of research is focused on bionic arms.

APPLY

A. Read these statements. Decide whether each one is a fact or an opinion. Write *Fact* or *Opinion* on the line. Compare answers with a partner.

_____ 1. *The Six Million Dollar Man* was a science-fiction TV show.

_____ 2. *Bionic* is a confusing term for people with artificial limbs.

_____ 3. It must be strange to have someone touch your chest and feel it in your hand.

_____ 4. Claudia is very lucky that she has a bionic arm.

_____ 5. Claudia's bionic arm is very heavy.

B. Look again at Reading 2. Scan the article to find one sentence that states an opinion. (Hint: It's about Claudia.)

C. In your notebook, write two facts and two opinions about the people in Reading 2. Read your sentences aloud in a small group and let the others decide which are facts and which are opinions. Discuss any statements that you disagree about.

Vocabulary Activities | STEP I: Word Level

A. With a partner, list some alternatives for these situations.

1. Your uncle was in a car accident and both of his legs were injured. Suggest some alternate ways for him to travel to his job.

2. Your grandmother's eyesight is very poor. She likes stories about famous people, but she can't see well enough to read. What alternatives can you suggest so she can still enjoy these stories?

B. *Confine* can mean to keep someone or something in a particular place. It can also refer to controlling or setting the limits of something. With a partner, match the type of business in the first column to what it confined (center column) and the type of limit (last column). In your notebook, take turns making sentences.

*This restaurant **confined** its menu to Mexican food.*

Type of Business	What It Confined	Type of Limit
1. ~~a restaurant~~	its broadcasting	girls under 18
2. a library	its children's books	~~Mexican food~~
3. a private school	its repairs	900 words
4. a clothing store	~~its menu~~	items under $20
5. an auto repair shop	its articles	Japanese cars
6. a radio station	its student body	a cozy corner
7. a magazine	merchandise	ten hours a day

Voluntary describes an action that is done willingly, without being required to do it.

The adverb form is *voluntarily*.

> *Involvement in the study is strictly **voluntary.** You don't have to do it to graduate.*
>
> *The participants **voluntarily** donated their time to help the researchers.*

The noun and the verb have the same form: *volunteer.*

> ***Volunteers** at the local hospital play games with the sick children.*
>
> *Amy always **volunteers** to help out when they are shorthanded.*

CORPUS

C. **With a partner, decide which of these actions are voluntary and which are required.**

1. giving your seat on a bus to an old person
2. straightening crooked teeth with braces
3. wearing glasses to improve your vision
4. getting a passport to travel overseas
5. using a bed net to prevent malaria
6. getting a license to drive a car
7. paying for groceries at a market
8. visiting a sick patient in a hospital

An *advocate* is a person who speaks or writes publicly in favor of a particular position or cause. *Advocacy* is the noun form of this action. The verb is also *advocate.*

> *My uncle is an **advocate** for disabled people. He **advocates** for them.*
>
> *His **advocacy** resulted in new laws to help the disabled.*

CORPUS

D. **Imagine that the city wants to build a new hospital. They asked doctors at the current hospital to volunteer ideas for the new hospital. Each doctor is an advocate for his or her own specialty. With a partner, match the doctor with what he or she might advocate. Take turns making sentences with the information. Check your dictionary for the meaning of new words.**

> *The surgeon is an **advocate** of doubling the number of operating rooms.*
>
> *The surgeon **advocates** doubling the number of operating rooms.*

___ 1. pediatrician   a. doubling the number of operating rooms

___ 2. pharmacist   b. installing reclining chairs for new mothers

___ 3. obstetrician   c. building a modern kitchen for the cafeteria

___ 4. nutritionist   d. building a playroom for the sick children

_a_ 5. surgeon   e. purchasing new X-ray machines

___ 6. radiologist   f. adding computers to keep track of medicines

To *suspend* <u>something</u> means to hang something, either permanently or temporarily.

> *Jesse's new arm was **suspended** from his shoulder by a plastic frame.*

To *suspend* <u>an activity</u> is to stop it temporarily.

> *The lab will **suspend** research on the vaccine until a new director is hired.*

To *suspend* <u>a person</u> is to dismiss them from a job, school, project, etc. temporarily, usually as a punishment. *Suspension* is the noun form.

> *Hannah was **suspended** from school for a week for bad behavior.*
>
> *During her **suspension** she wasn't allowed to watch TV or go online.*

CORPUS

E. Rewrite these sentences using a form of *suspend*. Compare your sentences with a partner.

1. The biology lab technician was dismissed for a week for being careless.
2. He hung hot lamps too close to the dishes of bacteria we were studying.
3. We had to stop our experiment until we could grow new bacteria.
4. The technician was not paid during the time he was not working.
5. When he returns, we'll show him the proper way to hang the lamps.

Word Form Chart			
Noun	**Verb**	**Adjective**	**Adverb**
proportion	_____	(dis)proportional (dis)proportionate	(dis)proportionally (dis)proportionately

A *proportion* is concerned with the relationship among the parts that make up a whole. Like a ratio, it can compare one part to another part in terms of number. It can also compare parts in terms of importance, size, degree, or other factors.

> *The largest **proportion** of undergraduates is made up of women.*

The two adjective forms are interchangeable, as are the two adverb forms.

> *An enormous TV took up a **disproportionally** large area of the room.*
>
> *Each roommate had a **proportionate** amount of space in the closet.*

When two parts are *in proportion,* this means they are of the correct sizes relative to each other. For instance, in an accurate drawing of a person, the ears will be larger than the eyes—but they are supposed to be. *Out of proportion* is the opposite.

> *The artist has drawn the eyes and ears in **proportion**.*
>
> *But look how big the mouth is. It's **out of proportion** with the rest of the head.*

CORPUS

F. The information in this activity has been taken from the first nine units of this book. In your notebook, restate the information using a form of *proportion*. Compare only their relative size or importance (no statistics necessary). Be prepared to read aloud and discuss your sentences in a small group.

1. The oceans of the world occupy over 70 percent of the earth's surface.

   *The oceans of the world occupy a large **proportion** of the earth's surface.*

2. Food from the sea provides between 5 percent and 10 percent of the total world food supply.

3. Of the earth's seven billion people, over one billion rely on fish as a primary source of protein.

4. Ambition seems to coincide most often with middle-class status.

5. Celebrities as a group are more narcissistic than other people.

6. Kids with autism are predominantly male, with boys outnumbering girls by a ratio of 4 to 1.

7. About 90 percent of the world's malaria deaths occur in sub-Saharan Africa.

8. As the rainforest disappears, so will the native people.

9. Hundreds of new gas stations were built along the highways, complemented by new fast-food restaurants.

10. Fast-Food Franchises in 2008: McDonald's 30,000; Burger King 11,550.

G. Self-Assessment Review: Go back to page 145 and reassess your knowledge of the target vocabulary. How has your understanding of the words changed? What words do you feel most comfortable with now?

Writing and Discussion Topics

With a partner or a small group, share ideas about the following topics. Then have each person write a paragraph about one of the topics.

1. Some people consider eyeglasses one of the most important inventions in human history. Do you agree or disagree? Why?

2. What devices do you know of that assist people who are blind? What devices do you know of that assist people who are deaf?

3. It is estimated that Claudia's bionic arm cost $4 million. Do you think this is a good investment for research dollars? Why or why not?

The Academic Word List

Words targeted in Level 1 are bold

Word	Sublist	Location
🔑 **abandon**	8	**L1, U7**
abstract	6	L3, U5
academy	5	L3, U1
🔑 **access**	4	**L1, U2**
accommodate	9	L2, U7
🔑 **accompany**	8	**L1, U2**
accumulate	8	L2, U4
🔑 accurate	6	L4, U6; L0, U2
🔑 achieve	2	L4, U1; L0, U9
🔑 **acknowledge**	6	**L1, U7**
🔑 **acquire**	2	**L1, U4**
🔑 adapt	7	L4, U7
🔑 adequate	4	L2, U4
adjacent	10	L2, U3
🔑 adjust	5	L4, U3
administrate	2	**L1, U3**
🔑 adult	7	L3, U6
advocate	7	**L1, U10**
🔑 affect	2	L2, U6; L0, U10
aggregate	6	**L1, U9**
🔑 aid	7	L2, U7
albeit	10	**L1, U7**
allocate	6	L2, U6
🔑 **alter**	5	**L1, U1**
🔑 **alternative**	3	**L1, U10**
🔑 **ambiguous**	8	**L1, U4**
amend	5	L2, U9
analogy	9	**L1, U4**
🔑 analyze	1	L2, U3; L0, U01
🔑 **annual**	4	**L1, U9**
🔑 anticipate	9	L2, U3
apparent	4	L2, U9
append	8	L2, U10
🔑 appreciate	8	L3, U5
🔑 approach	1	L3, U1; L0, U10
🔑 **appropriate**	2	**L1, U8**
🔑 approximate	4	L3, U4
arbitrary	8	L2, U8
🔑 area	1	L4, U1; L0, U5
🔑 aspect	2	L3, U4
assemble	10	L3, U10
assess	1	**L1, U8**
assign	6	L2, U9
🔑 assist	2	L2, U5; L0, U4
🔑 assume	1	L2, U1; L0, U4
🔑 assure	9	L3, U4
🔑 attach	6	L3, U7

Word	Sublist	Location
attain	9	L1, U5
🔑 attitude	4	L4, U6
attribute	4	L3, U10
🔑 author	6	L2, U4
🔑 **authority**	1	**L1, U6**
automate	8	L3, U6; L0, U7
🔑 available	1	L3, U5; L0, U6
🔑 **aware**	5	**L1, U5**
🔑 behalf	9	L3, U9
🔑 benefit	1	L4, U2; L0, U9
bias	8	L4, U8
🔑 bond	6	L4, U3
🔑 brief	6	L3, U6
bulk	9	L4, U9
🔑 **capable**	6	**L1, U8**
🔑 capacity	5	L4, U9
🔑 category	2	L4, U5
🔑 cease	9	L4, U10
🔑 challenge	5	L3, U8
🔑 **channel**	7	**L1, U3**
🔑 chapter	2	L3, U7
🔑 chart	8	L3, U10
🔑 chemical	7	L2, U10
🔑 circumstance	3	L2, U10; L0, U8
cite	6	L4, U10
🔑 **civil**	4	**L1, U4**
clarify	8	L4, U8
🔑 classic	7	L3, U9
clause	5	L2, U8
🔑 code	4	L4, U9
coherent	9	L2, U5
coincide	9	**L1, U5**
🔑 collapse	10	L4, U10
🔑 **colleague**	10	**L1, U5**
commence	9	L3, U9
🔑 comment	3	L3, U3
🔑 commission	2	L3, U9
🔑 commit	4	L2, U6; L0, U8
commodity	8	L4, U6
🔑 communicate	4	L3, U2
🔑 community	2	L2, U7; L0, U4
compatible	9	**L1, U9**
compensate	3	L3, U4
compile	10	L2, U6
complement	8	**L1, U7**

Word	Sublist	Location
🔑 complex	2	L4, U2; L0, U1
🔑 component	3	L4, U3
compound	5	L4, U6
comprehensive	7	L2, U7
comprise	7	L4, U9
compute	2	L4, U8
conceive	10	L4, U10
🔑 concentrate	4	L3, U8
🔑 concept	1	L3, U1; L0, U10
🔑 **conclude**	2	**L1, U6**
concurrent	9	L4, U5
🔑 **conduct**	2	**L1, U9**
confer	4	L4, U4
confine	9	**L1, U10**
🔑 confirm	7	L4, U10
🔑 **conflict**	5	**L1, U2**
conform	8	L4, U7
consent	3	L4, U7
consequent	2	L2, U3; L0, U4
🔑 considerable	3	L3, U8
🔑 consist	1	L4, U2, U9; L0, U7
🔑 constant	3	L4, U8
constitute	1	**L1, U4**
constrain	3	**L1, U8**
🔑 construct	2	L3, U1; L0, U5
🔑 **consult**	5	**L1, U6**
consume	2	L2, U2; L0, U10
🔑 contact	5	L2, U10
🔑 **contemporary**	8	**L1, U7**
🔑 **context**	1	**L1, U4**
🔑 contract	1	L3, U9
contradict	8	L2, U2
contrary	7	**L1, U6**
🔑 **contrast**	4	**L1, U7**
🔑 **contribute**	3	**L1, U9**
controversy	9	L2, U3
convene	3	**L1, U4**
converse	9	L2, U8
🔑 convert	7	L2, U2
🔑 **convince**	10	**L1, U3**
cooperate	6	**L1, U2**
coordinate	3	L2, U6
🔑 core	3	L2, U5
corporate	3	L2, U2
correspond	3	L3, U9
🔑 couple	7	L3, U1
🔑 create	1	L2, U1; L0, U1

🔑 Oxford 3000™ words

Word	Sublist	Location
credit	2	L3, U6
criteria	3	L3, U3
crucial	8	L3, U10
culture	2	L4, U10; L0, U6
currency	8	L3, U9
cycle	4	L4, U5
data	1	L2, U3; L0, U10
debate	4	L2, U4
decade	**7**	**L1, U7**
decline	**5**	**L1, U2**
deduce	3	L4, U7
define	1	L3, U2; L0, U4
definite	7	L3, U4
demonstrate	**3**	**L1, U5**
denote	8	L4, U6
deny	7	L4, U10
depress	10	L2, U4
derive	1	L4, U10; L0, U10
design	**2**	**L1, U1; L0, U5**
despite	4	L3, U2
detect	**8**	**L1, U6**
deviate	8	L2, U8
device	9	L2, U3
devote	9	L3, U9
differentiate	**7**	**L1, U4**
dimension	4	L4, U5
diminish	9	L4, U4
discrete	5	L2, U6
discriminate	**6**	**L1, U10**
displace	8	L2, U7
display	6	L3, U5; L0, U8
dispose	7	L4, U6
distinct	2	L3, U7
distort	9	L3, U6
distribute	1	L4, U8
diverse	6	L2, U8
document	3	L4, U9
domain	6	L2, U8
domestic	**4**	**L1, U3**
dominate	**3**	**L1, U5**
draft	5	L3, U6
drama	8	L3, U5
duration	9	L4, U1
dynamic	**7**	**L1, U5**
economy	**1**	**L1, U7**
edit	6	L4, U8
element	2	L4, U1
eliminate	7	L2, U9
emerge	4	L2, U1

Word	Sublist	Location
emphasis	3	L2, U9
empirical	7	L3, U4
enable	5	L3, U10
encounter	10	L3, U5
energy	5	L2, U5
enforce	5	L4, U7
enhance	6	L3, U1
enormous	10	L3, U8
ensure	3	L2, U5; L0, U6
entity	5	L4, U5
environment	1	L2, U1; L3, U8; L0, U3
equate	2	L2, U2
equip	7	L2, U3
equivalent	5	L3, U10
erode	**9**	**L1, U9**
error	**4**	**L1, U10**
establish	**1**	**L1, U6**
estate	6	L4, U6
estimate	1	L2, U10
ethic	9	L2, U9
ethnic	4	L2, U1; L3, U3
evaluate	**2**	**L1, U10**
eventual	8	L4, U3
evident	1	L4, U2; L0, U8
evolve	5	L2, U7
exceed	6	L4, U1
exclude	3	L4, U7
exhibit	8	L2, U5
expand	**5**	**L1, U7**
expert	6	L3, U8
explicit	**6**	**L1, U3**
exploit	**8**	**L1, U5**
export	**1**	**L1, U3**
expose	5	L3, U5
external	5	L2, U10
extract	7	L3, U2
facilitate	5	L4, U1
factor	1	L3, U8; L0, U4
feature	2	L4, U1; L0, U2
federal	6	L2, U3
fee	**6**	**L1, U1**
file	7	L4, U6
final	2	L4, U3
finance	1	L2, U2
finite	**7**	**L1, U9**
flexible	6	L3, U9
fluctuate	8	L2, U7
focus	2	L3, U8
format	9	L4, U8

Word	Sublist	Location
formula	1	L4, U8
forthcoming	10	L4, U3
found	9	L4, U8
foundation	7	L4, U4
framework	**3**	**L1, U1**
function	1	L3, U1
fund	3	L3, U3
fundamental	5	L4, U4
furthermore	6	L4, U9
gender	6	L2, U8
generate	**5**	**L1, U5**
generation	**5**	**L1, U7**
globe	7	L3, U2
goal	4	L3, U3
grade	**7**	**L1, U7**
grant	4	L2, U9
guarantee	7	L2, U8
guideline	8	L3, U3
hence	4	L3, U5
hierarchy	7	L3, U4
highlight	8	L4, U3
hypothesis	4	L4, U7
identical	7	L4, U5
identify	1	L4, U2; L0, U7
ideology	7	L4, U6
ignorance	6	L2, U9
illustrate	3	L4, U9
image	5	L3, U5
immigrate	3	L2, U1
impact	**2**	**L1, U9**
implement	**4**	**L1, U2**
implicate	4	L4, U7
implicit	**8**	**L1, U3**
imply	3	L4, U7
impose	**4**	**L1, U10**
incentive	**6**	**L1, U10**
incidence	6	L3, U10
incline	**10**	**L1, U7**
income	**1**	**L1, U3**
incorporate	6	L4, U4
index	**6**	**L1, U4**
indicate	1	L2, U4; L0, U10
individual	**1**	**L1, U1**
induce	8	L3, U7
inevitable	8	L2, U8
infer	**7**	**L1, U8**
infrastructure	8	L4, U6
inherent	**9**	**L1, U1**

Oxford 3000™ words

Word	Sublist	Location
inhibit	6	L1, U5
initial	3	L3, U7; L0, U8
initiate	6	L2, U10
injure	2	L1, U1
innovate	7	L1, U3
input	6	L3, U6
insert	7	L2, U9
insight	9	L3, U7
inspect	8	L3, U3
instance	3	L1, U6
institute	2	L2, U8
instruct	6	L4, U2
integral	9	L1, U4
integrate	4	L2, U7
integrity	10	L3, U7
intelligence	6	L3, U8
intense	8	L1, U2
interact	3	L1, U8
intermediate	9	L2, U7
internal	4	L3, U7
interpret	1	L3, U3
interval	6	L2, U5
intervene	7	L2, U8
intrinsic	10	L4, U4
invest	2	L2, U4
investigate	4	L4, U8
invoke	10	L1, U3
involve	1	L2, U3
isolate	7	L3, U4
issue	1	L4, U2; L0, U8
item	2	L3, U10; L0, U7
job	4	L1, U1
journal	2	L2, U6
justify	3	L2, U3
label	4	L2, U2
labor	1	L1, U2
layer	3	L3, U4
lecture	6	L4, U2
legal	1	L2, U3
legislate	1	L3, U3
levy	10	L2, U9
liberal	5	L2, U1
license	5	L3, U9
likewise	10	L4, U5
link	3	L1, U8; L0, U1
locate	3	L2, U1; L0, U1
logic	5	L1, U6
maintain	2	L4, U1; L0, U9

Word	Sublist	Location
major	1	L3, U2; L0, U5
manipulate	8	L4, U4
manual	9	L3, U10
margin	5	L4, U3
mature	9	L1, U8
maximize	3	L2, U8
mechanism	4	L3, U9
media	7	L1, U5
mediate	9	L4, U2
medical	5	L1, U2
medium	9	L2, U2
mental	5	L2, U6
method	1	L4, U9
migrate	6	L3, U2
military	9	L1, U4
minimal	9	L2, U10
minimize	8	L1, U1
minimum	6	L4, U5
ministry	6	L1, U2
minor	3	L3, U7
mode	7	L4, U7
modify	5	L2, U3
monitor	5	L2, U3
motive	6	L1, U6
mutual	9	L3, U3
negate	3	L4, U2
network	5	L3, U2
neutral	6	L2, U10
nevertheless	6	L4, U10
nonetheless	10	L4, U7
norm	9	L4, U6
normal	2	L3, U8; L4, U2
notion	5	L4, U9
notwithstanding	10	L2, U1
nuclear	8	L2, U7
objective	5	L1, U10
obtain	2	L3, U6; L0, U10
obvious	4	L3, U7
occupy	4	L1, U9
occur	1	L1, U2
odd	10	L1, U8
offset	8	L4, U8
ongoing	10	L3, U3
option	4	L4, U7
orient	5	L2, U5
outcome	3	L3, U4
output	4	L1, U7
overall	4	L2, U6
overlap	9	L1, U7

Word	Sublist	Location
overseas	6	L1, U1
panel	10	L1, U6
paradigm	7	L2, U6
paragraph	8	L3, U6
parallel	4	L3, U9
parameter	4	L4, U5
participate	2	L1, U8
partner	3	L3, U1
passive	9	L2, U8
perceive	2	L2, U9
percent	1	L2, U10
period	1	L2, U6
persist	10	L2, U4
perspective	5	L3, U2
phase	4	L1, U8
phenomenon	7	L2, U5
philosophy	3	L4, U5
physical	3	L4, U4; L0, U4
plus	8	L4, U5
policy	1	L3, U3
portion	9	L3, U9
pose	10	L3, U1
positive	2	L1, U5
potential	2	L4, U8; L0, U10
practitioner	8	L1, U2
precede	6	L2, U4
precise	5	L3, U10
predict	4	L2, U1
predominant	8	L1, U8
preliminary	9	L4, U1
presume	6	L2, U2
previous	2	L2, U5; L0, U5
primary	2	L1, U1
prime	5	L4, U4
principal	4	L4, U5
principle	1	L3, U9; L0, U9
prior	4	L3, U6
priority	7	L1, U2
proceed	1	L4, U9; L0, U3
process	1	L1, U9
professional	4	L1, U5
prohibit	7	L3, U10
project	4	L4, U4,U9
promote	4	L2, U6
proportion	3	L1, U10
prospect	8	L2, U6
protocol	9	L2, U4
psychology	5	L4, U2
publication	7	L3, U1
publish	3	L1, U3

Word	Sublist	Location	Word	Sublist	Location	Word	Sublist	Location
purchase	2	L2, U9; L0, U7	secure	2	L4, U6; L0, U8	**terminate**	8	**L1, U9**
pursue	5	L3, U8	seek	2	L4, U3; L0, U4	text	2	L2, U4
			select	2	L3, U1	theme	8	L2, U2
qualitative	9	L3, U9	sequence	3	L3, U5	theory	1	L4, U4; L0, U9
quote	7	L4, U10	series	4	L3, U5	thereby	8	L4, U3
			sex	3	**L1, U3**	thesis	7	L4, U7
radical	8	L3, U4	shift	3	L4, U9; L0, U2	topic	7	L3, U3
random	8	L2, U7	significant	1	L3, U10; L0, U6	**trace**	6	**L1, U9**
range	2	L3, U1	similar	1	L2, U1; L0, U2	tradition	2	L3, U6; L0, U4
ratio	5	**L1, U8**	simulate	7	L3, U1	transfer	2	L4, U1; L0, U3
rational	6	L3, U3	**site**	2	**L1, U6**	transform	6	L2, U7
react	3	L2, U6; L0, U3	so-called	10	L2, U8	transit	5	L3, U5
recover	6	L3, U4	sole	7	L4, U1	transmit	7	L4, U4
refine	9	L4, U4	**somewhat**	7	**L1, U4**	transport	6	L4, U10; L0, U9
regime	4	L2, U10	source	1	L3, U2; L0, U10	trend	5	L4, U6
region	2	L3, U1	**specific**	1	**L1, U6**	trigger	9	L3, U7
register	3	L2, U2	specify	3	L4, U6			
regulate	2	L3, U6; L0, U9	sphere	9	L3, U7	**ultimate**	7	**L1, U9**
reinforce	8	L2, U5	stable	5	L4, U5	undergo	10	L4, U1
reject	5	**L1, U7**	statistic	4	L4, U7	underlie	6	L4, U6
relax	9	**L1, U8**	status	4	L3, U2	undertake	4	L2, U3
release	7	L4, U1	straightforward	10	L3, U4	uniform	8	L3, U1
relevant	2	L4, U8	strategy	2	L2, U5; L0, U9	unify	9	L4, U5
reluctance	10	L2, U4	stress	4	L4, U4	unique	7	L2, U1; L0, U7
rely	3	L3, U2; L0, U6	structure	1	L2, U1; L0, U5	utilize	6	L3, U8
remove	3	L3, U2; L0, U8	**style**	5	**L1, U4**			
require	1	L4, U2; L0, U9	submit	7	L2, U9	valid	3	L4, U10
research	1	L4, U2	subordinate	9	L4, U3	vary	1	L3, U10; L0, U2
reside	2	**L1, U2**	**subsequent**	4	**L1, U1**	vehicle	8	L4, U3
resolve	4	L3, U4	subsidy	6	L2, U2	version	5	L3, U5
resource	2	L3, U8	**substitute**	5	**L1, U1**	**via**	8	**L1, U4**
respond	1	L4, U7	successor	7	L2, U9	violate	9	L3, U6
restore	8	L3, U5	sufficient	3	L2, U10; L0, U4	virtual	8	L2, U10
restrain	9	L2, U7	**sum**	4	**L1, U10**	visible	7	L3, U5
restrict	2	L2, U9; L0, U6	summary	4	L2, U10	vision	9	L4, U3
retain	4	L4, U3	supplement	9	L4, U10	visual	8	L3, U7
reveal	6	L3, U8	**survey**	2	**L1, U3**	volume	3	L2, U4
revenue	5	L2, U2	survive	7	L3, U2	**voluntary**	7	**L1, U10**
reverse	7	L2, U7	**suspend**	9	**L1, U10**	welfare	5	L4, U1
revise	8	L3, U6	sustain	5	L2, U4	whereas	5	L4, U2
revolution	9	**L1, U1**	symbol	5	L2, U2	**whereby**	10	**L1, U4**
rigid	9	L2, U7				widespread	8	L4, U10
role	1	**L1, U5**	**tape**	6	**L1, U6**			
route	9	L2, U5	target	5	L3, U10			
			team	9	L2, U6			
scenario	9	L3, U7	**technical**	3	**L1, U6**			
schedule	8	L4, U9	technique	3	L2, U1; L0, U6			
scheme	3	L4, U3	technology	3	L3, U8; L0, U7			
scope	6	L4, U8	**temporary**	9	**L1, U9**			
section	1	L2, U5	tense	8	**L1, U10**			
sector	1	**L1, U3**						

🔑 Oxford 3000™ words